How to Think Like Aquinas

Kevin Vost, Psy.D.

# HOW TO
# THINK LIKE
# AQUINAS

## THE SURE WAY TO PERFECT
## YOUR MENTAL POWERS

SOPHIA INSTITUTE PRESS
Manchester, New Hampshire

Scripture quotations have been taken from the Catholic Edition of the Revised Standard Version of the Bible (RSV), copyright © 1965 and 1966 by the Division of Christian Education of the National Council of the Churches of Christ in the United States of America. Used by permission. All rights reserved.

Excerpts from the English translation of the Catechism of the Catholic Church for use in the United States of America, copyright © 1994 by United States Catholic Conference, Inc.–Libreria Editrice Vaticana. Used with permission.

Sophia Institute Press
Box 5284, Manchester, NH 03108
1-800-888-9344

www.SophiaInstitute.com

Sophia Institute Press® is a registered trademark of Sophia Institute.

**Library of Congress Cataloging-in-Publication Data**

Names: Vost, Kevin, author.
Title: How to think like Aquinas : the sure way to perfect your mental powers / Kevin Vost.
Description: Manchester, New Hampshire : Sophia Institute Press, 2018.
    Includes bibliographical references.
Identifiers: LCCN 2018029093   ISBN 9781622825066 (pbk. : alk. paper)
Subjects: LCSH: Thomas, Aquinas, Saint, 1225?-1274. Thought and thinking.
Classification: LCC B765.T54 V67 2018   DDC 230/.2092 — dc23 LC record available at https://lccn.loc.gov/2018029093

First printing

*To all Thomists of every stripe, who through prayer,
study, reading, teaching, preaching, writing, or one-on-one
conversation strive to share with others the
heavenly wisdom of the Angelic Doctor*

# Contents

## Part 2

## FATHOMING THE DEPTHS OF WISDOM

How to Think Like Aquinas

# Why You Should Think Like Aquinas (and How)

*He alone enlightened the Church more than all other doctors; a man can derive more profit from his books in one year than from pondering all his life the teaching of others.* [1]

—Pope John XXII

*The human soul is the highest and noblest of forms. Wherefore it excels corporeal matter in its power by the fact that it has an operation and a power in which corporeal matter has no share whatsoever. This power is called the intellect.*

—St. Thomas Aquinas, *Summa Theologica*, I, Q. 76, art. 2

## Why Should You Think Like Aquinas?

We should all strive to think more like Aquinas, but only if we desire to know what is true, to love what is good, to grow in happiness and holiness while wayfarers on earth, and ultimately to share in eternal beatitude with God and the communion of

---

[1] As cited in Pope Pius IX, motu proprio *Doctoris Angelici* (June 29, 1914).

saints when we arrive home in heaven. You see, in all of human history, St. Thomas Aquinas (1225–1274) was among the very best guides to fulfilling these desires. Dozens of popes have sung his praises as philosopher and theologian, the *Catechism of the Catholic Church* abounds in references to his writings, and even secular scholars have acknowledged his monumental contribution to the field of philosophy.[2] They praise him foremost for what G. K. Chesterton called in his biography of Thomas "that unusual human hobby: the habit of thinking."[3]

Of course, by thinking *like* Aquinas I do not pretend to possess the keys to thinking *as well as* St. Thomas (as much as I wish I did!). Thomas was gifted with a uniquely powerful intellect and was quite aware that God gives some of us more powerful potential for greater depths of thinking than He gives others: "Experience shows that some understand more profoundly than do others; as one who carries a conclusion to its first principles and ultimate causes understands it better than one who reduces it to its proximate causes."[4]

Many centuries later, groups of modern psychologists have concluded repeatedly that the capacity for higher-level "abstract thinking" (the stuff of "first principles and ultimate causes") is a

---

[2] See Charles A. Murray, *Human Accomplishment: The Pursuit of Excellence in the Arts and Sciences, 800 BC to 1950* (New York: HarperCollins, 2003). In this book, Murray, an agnostic, lists St. Thomas among the "giants" of Western philosophy, ranking him the sixth most influential of all time—above Socrates and St. Augustine. Note that philosophy was not Thomas's specialty, but merely a tool—a "handmaiden" to theology, the highest of all branches of learning.

[3] G. K. Chesterton, *Saint Thomas Aquinas: The Dumb Ox* (New York: Doubleday Image, 1956), 80.

[4] Aquinas, *Summa Theologica*, I, Q. 85, art. 7.

fundamental hallmark of human intelligence. So, Thomas truly understood *the nature of thinking* and *the habits required to perfect it*. He was blessed with a uniquely powerful intelligence able to fathom the most ultimate of causes and principles. Further, he possessed the capacity to enlighten others by making the abstract more concrete, by capturing lofty truths and bringing them down to earth, so that the average person could grab onto them firmly and be raised up by them.

Regardless of how you might think of yourself as a thinker, Thomas is a most trustworthy guide for helping you to maximize your unique God-given capacities to think and reason about the things that matter most to you. Further, whoever has the capacity to read and understand these pages has the capacity to improve greatly his powers of thinking—indeed, to grow adept at that most "unusual hobby" and think more like Aquinas!

Perhaps more than ever, we need to develop our capacities for clear thought on the things that always matter the most, such as the existence and the nature of God and how we should live our lives and relate to our Church, families, neighbors, and fellow citizens.

We live in a day when many young people declare themselves "nones" (people with no religious affiliation)[5] amidst a barrage of propaganda that people who value thinking should choose *reason and science* over *faith and religion*, with the latter presented

[5] In 2014, the Pew Research Center found that 22.8 percent of more than thirty-five thousand American adults polled about their religious beliefs identified themselves as either atheist, agnostic, or "nothing in particular," up from 16.1 percent only seven years before. Michael Lipka, "10 Facts About Atheists," Pew Research Center, June 1, 2016, http://www.pewresearch.org/fact-tank/2016/06/01/10-facts-about-atheists/.

as matters of blind belief, sentimental tradition, and remnants of primitive superstition.

In our time, St. John Paul II stated elegantly how faith and reason, properly understood, are not at all opposed, but "are like two wings on which the human spirit rises to the contemplation of truth."[6] Nearly eight centuries ago, St. Thomas Aquinas, the "Angelic Doctor," showed us many ways to obtain maximum lift from both of those wings, and that is what this book is about.

As for what we might call the "wing of reason," Thomas knew well that the powers of thought that arise from our human nature are "also aided by art and diligence."[7] In other words, intelligent thought and accurate thinking are not just capacities that you and I have in some fixed measure but are flexible potentials that can be built, improved, and actualized by training and practice ("diligence") in the right methods ("art" being short for "artificial" or man-made). Your powers of memory, for example, or of logical reasoning, are fluid capacities that *you can build and improve by using them in the right ways.* As we proceed through this book we will learn the ways provided in the writings of St. Thomas—and practice them as we go!

As for the "wing of faith," Thomas knew as well that "grace does not destroy nature but perfects it; natural reason should minister to faith as the natural bent of the will ministers to charity."[8] Further, "when a man's will is ready to believe, he loves the truth he believes; he thinks out and takes to heart whatever reasons he

---

[6] Pope John Paul II, encyclical letter *Fides et Ratio* (September 14, 1998), preamble. Pope Benedict XVI spoke as well of the "friendship" of reason and faith in his papal address of March 24, 2010.

[7] *Summa Theologica*, II-II, Q. 49, art. 1.

[8] Ibid., I, Q. 1, art. 8.

can find in support thereof; and in this way human reason does not exclude the merit of faith but is a sign of greater merit."[9]

Clearly then, Thomas knew that God gave us reason for a reason — to find truth in the world around us and to serve the faith that will guide us to Truth in eternity. It is up to us, then, to build on our natural thinking capacities both by developing and practicing the arts that perfect them on a natural plane, and by becoming more open to the graces from above that will raise them to heavenly heights.

### How Can You Think Like Aquinas?

We can all come to think more like Aquinas in three steps:

1. By *reading and reflecting* on what he wrote specifically about thinking, study, and the nature of perfection of the human intellect
2. By *observing the methods of thinking* St. Thomas employed in his great writings, such as his over-three-million-word *Summa Theologica* and many others
3. By *practicing what he preached and taught* through simple exercises included throughout this book

As for the first step, our guiding template for this book will be the brief, elegant, delightful "Letter of St. Thomas to Brother John on How to Study." We will examine this extraordinary letter in its entirety, fleshing out our reflections (in keeping with step two) with insights drawn from St. Thomas's massive body of other great works and from works of great modern-day Thomists, students of the philosophical and theological wisdom of St. Thomas Aquinas. We will also mine some important events from Thomas's life story to see how he lived out the principles he taught others.

---

[9] Ibid., I-II, Q. 1, art. 10.

As for step three, each chapter will conclude with simple "Read, Reflect, and Remember" exercises designed to help us absorb, retain, and expand upon each chapter's golden nuggets of wisdom from St. Thomas.[10]

What better place than our introduction to dive into the introduction to Thomas's letter to Brother John? Here we go:

### On Sailing Your Way toward a Treasure Trove of Knowledge

This letter's authenticity, as having been penned by St. Thomas, has been questioned by some. We don't know, for example, who this Brother John was or when the letter was written. Still, Thomas was known to take time from his prodigious writing, teaching, and preaching duties to respond to letters requesting his advice. Further, commentators, including Father White and Father Sertillanges, note that its content is quite consistent with statements found in Thomas's other writings.[11] This letter's *worth*, then, is unquestionable for those who would strive

---

[10] Pope Leo XIII exhorted the Church to "restore the golden wisdom of Thomas and to spread it far and wide for the defense and beauty of the Catholic Faith, for the good of society, and for the advantage of all the sciences." See Pope Leo XIII, encyclical *Aeterni Patris* (August 4, 1879).

[11] Thomas's brief letter can be found online in various formats and translations. I found the original Latin and an English translation in a wonderful little book by St. Thomas Aquinas and Victor White, *How to Study: Being the Letter of St. Thomas Aquinas to Brother John, De Modo Studendi* (Oxford: Oxonian Press, 1953). An English translation also appears spread throughout the chapters of A. G. Sertillanges and Mary Ryan, *The Intellectual Life: Its Spirit, Conditions, Methods* (Westminster, MD: Newman Press, 1948).

to think like Aquinas! Let's dive in now and reflect on it. Here is its introduction:

> Because you have asked me, Brother John, most dear to me in Christ, how to set about acquiring the treasure of knowledge, this is my advice to you; namely, that you should choose to enter by small rivers, and not go straight into the sea; for difficult things should be reached by way of easy things. Such is therefore my advice on your way of life.

The first lesson to be gleaned is that to think like Aquinas is to center one's thoughts and affections on Jesus Christ. A second lesson is that knowledge is indeed a rightful treasure to be sought by the followers of Christ. Christ declared that what we treasure reveals our heart's desires and we should seek not earthly, but heavenly treasures (see Matt. 6:19–21). Clearly, then, to seek truth is a proper desire and one that will be fulfilled completely with the Beatific Vision of God, who is Truth.[12] In the meanwhile, here on earth, to obtain truth requires both the sweat of our brows and application of the right methods.

Thomas reveals that the first of those methods is to approach the vast sea of knowledge via smaller, more navigable streams. We learn new things by comparing and contrasting them with

---

[12] Truth from the human perspective is the correspondence between reality and our understanding of it, conformity between thing and thought. Not only do created things conform or correspond to God's thought, but "His act of understanding is the measure and cause of every other being and intellect." Truth does not merely exist *in* God, as it can in us, but "He is truth itself, and the sovereign and first truth." Aquinas, *Summa Theologica*, I, Q. 16, art. 5.

things we already know, thereby widening the channels of our knowledge, bit by bit. We see this, for example, in the way we first learn the names of numbers and how to count before we move to addition, subtraction, multiplication, and division, and onto higher mathematical functions such as algebra, geometry, and such. Who could possibly survive the deep seas of calculus without having reached it via those ever-widening streams? Further, we navigate these streams and reach broader, deeper channels by following the guidance of our teachers, who have traveled much farther upstream than we have.

That is all common sense, but Voltaire said that "common sense is not so common," and ironically, we often see the lack of it in many of his modern heirs who criticize Christ and His Church. By this I refer to some modern atheists who navigate their way up the rivers of knowledge in their own specialty areas, such as mathematics or biology, but then dive right into the oceans of philosophy and theology with no conception of how far they are out of their depth! But that's another story, one that we'll examine a bit later in this book.

For now, let us note that Thomas's advice in his letter concerns not merely study, but a "way of life." In the rest of this book we will sail up those streams of knowledge and drink in the rest of his advice, so that we too might think like Aquinas, for to think like Aquinas is to strive to *live out* the truth that we seek, in imitation of the One who is "the way, and the truth, and the life" (John 14:6).

### On Fathoming Deeper Truths

The goal of each of the ten chapters in this book's first part is to help us sail up those small streams of learning toward vast seas of knowledge, with "Captain" St. Thomas at the ship's helm. Hopefully all will find it a pleasant trip with few difficulties to cause any intellectual seasickness. But we'll go a little further in this book's second part, for those who would care to try their ships upon the open seas. These seas are indeed fraught with dangers, for they take us into the realm of abstract thoughts, universal ideas, premises, arguments, and conclusions that threaten to sink so many people's ships in our day. This will be the stuff of our last three heftier chapters in the second half of this book.

Thomas wrote extensively in his many works about the nature, importance, and perfection of human reason. The virtue of prudence, or of "practical wisdom," for instance, he described as "right reason applied to action." Well, part of right reasoning is to know how to identify wrong reasoning when you see it! Chapter 11 consists of twenty common logical fallacies, which we will examine after touching briefly on the nature of reason itself and on the story of how the power of St. Thomas's reason made him the hero of a popular twentieth-century science-fiction story! Chapter 12 exposes twenty erroneous philosophical and ethical assumptions, worldviews, ideologies, or isms that wreak havoc in our world today, and chapter 13 comprises ten heresies and half-truths that have besieged Catholics over the centuries, some of which are still alive though unwell in our time.

We can consider the fallacies in chapter 11 as *affronts to logic*; the errors in chapter 12 as *affronts to philosophy* as a whole, and specifically to metaphysics (the study of being), epistemology (the study of how we know), and ethics (the study of moral behavior); and the heresies and half-truths in chapter 13 as *affronts to the Faith*, mistakes at least or attacks at most regarding the nature of Christ, the Holy Trinity, the Blessed Mother, and the Catholic Church.

Following Thomas's lead, we will address ways to dissect the kinds of logical fallacies, erroneous isms, and heresies and half-truths that have plagued our world in the past and continue to do so.

### Extra Helps for Thinking More Like Aquinas

*Doctor's Orders*: The "Doctor" here is the "Angelic Doctor," St. Thomas Aquinas, of course. In these brief essays, you will encounter prescriptions, some directly from the "prescription pad" of St. Thomas's writings, on how to develop the virtue examined in each chapter. Sections labeled "Reflect," "Read," and "Remember" include exercises to enhance your ability to remember all the essential lessons in this book, to guide you to resources for further learning, and to help you practice your God-given intellectual powers so that you may truly think more like Aquinas.

*Mnemonic Master Memory Table*: Oh yes, and lest I forget: the appendix provides in one handy master table a written summary of the memory exercises that appear throughout the second half of this book. (If you read along carefully and do all the exercises as you go through this book's chapters, by the time you get to this table, you may find that you do not need it!)

I will note as well that we will focus throughout on practical thinking and the perfection of study habits. I include practical, real-world examples of these thinking principles from the lives of St. Thomas, other saints and sages, and at times from my own life experiences (the life that I am most acquainted with).

So then, with the Angelic Doctor as our guide, let's get down to business to see how we can attain greater happiness and holiness through the perfection of our intellectual powers that can come from thinking like Aquinas.

## Part 1

# Navigating the Small Streams of Knowledge

*Chapter 1*

# Speak Slowly and Carry a Big Heart and Mind

*Be slow to speak, and slow to enter the com-
mon room where people chat.*

## Docility: The Willingness to Be Taught

Who better to learn how to learn from than one of the world's greatest teachers and the patron saint of scholars? Thomas, echoing Aristotle, wrote that "a characteristic of one possessing science is the ability to teach."[13] This is because a learner is "in potency" to learning; that is, he has an active, yet unrealized, *potential* to acquire new knowledge, but he must be led to that knowledge by someone in whom it is already *actualized*, someone who already knows what the student is trying to learn. Not only was Thomas's own potential for learning certainly unusual, and perhaps unsurpassed, but he was always extremely docile, that

---

[13] St. Thomas Aquinas and Aristotle, *Commentary on the Nicoma-chean Ethics* (Notre Dame, IN: Dumb Ox Books, 1993), 366. "Science" is used in the broadest sense here, synonymous with "knowledge," from the Latin *scire*, "to know."

is, willing to learn from others, for "docility" derives from the Latin *docere* — to teach.

Docility seems to have lost its connection to the willingness to be taught and has connotations of passivity and subservience, something to be avoided. But Thomas's docility could not have been more vibrant and active. He sought knowledge about the highest of things and sought out the very best teachers, both those living, such as his mentor St. Albert the Great, and those no longer living, such as the greatest philosophers and Church Fathers who lived before him, most notably St. Augustine and Aristotle, whose names and writings appear hundreds of times in the *Summa Theologica*.

Thomas's greatest teacher of all, however, was Jesus Christ, the God-Man and the "most excellent of teachers," who taught not through writings but in "that manner of teaching whereby His doctrine is imprinted on the hearts of His hearers" and "as one having power" through the words and deeds of His life.[14]

Thomas not only devoured the teaching of his human mentors but also digested, altered, corrected, and improved them at times, making the truths that they discovered his own through a lifetime of thought and experience. It was his lifelong zeal as a student, along with the grace of God, that rewarded Thomas with the knowledge and wisdom that equipped him so well to teach others.

Let's examine in this chapter, then, a few ways he can teach us all to yearn to learn and to acquire the kind of knowledge that someday might turn us all into some manner of teachers — those who help spread the golden wisdom of St. Thomas Aquinas, full

---

[14] Aquinas, *Summa Theologica*, III, Q. 42, a. 4, citing Matt. 7:29.

of valuable nuggets culled not only from the earth, but from the Good News of that greatest of teachers, Jesus Christ.

First, we will look at the brief letter St. Thomas wrote when Brother John asked him for study tips; then we'll explore the depths of meaning in his first simple precept: "Be slow to speak, and slow to enter the common room where people chat."

### *A Letter of St. Thomas to Brother John on How to Study*[15]

Because you have asked me, Brother John, most dear to me in Christ, how to set about acquiring the treasure of knowledge, this is my advice to you; namely, that you should choose to enter by small rivers, and not go straight into the sea; for difficult things should be reached by way of easy things. Such is therefore my advice on your way of life:

- Be slow to speak, and slow to enter the common room where people chat.
- Hold fast to purity of conscience.
- Do not cease to make time for prayer.
- Love to be frequently in your cell, if you wish to be admitted to the wine cellar.

---

[15] I put this English version together after reviewing the original Latin text in Father White's aforementioned book, along with his translation and other translations available online. The twelve bulleted precepts are addressed in order in each chapter of this book, though the second and third precepts, as well as the fifth and the seventh, are combined in this book's chapters 2 and 4 because of their close interconnections. That simplifies things a bit and leaves us with a nice round ten chapters of reasonable length.

- Show yourself amiable to everybody, or at least try; but become overly familiar with no one, for familiarity breeds contempt and introduces complications that will impede study.
- Also, do not get enmeshed in the words and deeds of worldly people.
- Above all, flee from aimless conversations.
- Do not fail to imitate the lives of saintly and noble men.
- Do not place value on who says what, but rather, commit to your memory what true things are said.
- Try to understand whatever you read and to verify whatever is doubtful.
- Put whatever you learn in the cupboard of your mind as if you were filling a cup to the brim.
- "Seek not the things that are too high for thee."[16]

Follow in the footsteps of blessed Dominic, who brought forth useful and wonderful leaves, flowers, and fruits in the vineyard of the Lord of Hosts for as long as life was his fellow traveler. If you shall have followed these steps, you will be able to attain whatever you desire. Farewell!

### On the Benefits of Engaging the Intellect before the Tongue

We covered Thomas's introductory paragraph in our introduction. His first piece of advice — "be slow to speak" — recalls the old maxim "Still waters run deep." There is certainly a sense in which each of Thomas's precepts are commonplaces, ordinary bits of advice embodying the kind of common sense that

---

[16] Sir. 3:21. "Seek not what is too difficult for you" in the RSVCE.

experienced parents or grandparents might share. Perhaps your parents or grandparents even told you long ago that God gave us *two* ears and only *one* mouth! Well, there is good reason that such maxims become common over time. Indeed, we are at risk if we should ever forget them. "The world is in danger for lack of life-giving maxims," wrote Father Sertillanges a few generations ago.[17] This first bit of wisdom is scriptural as well: "Be quick to hear, slow to speak (James 1:19); "Even a fool who keeps silent is considered wise; when he closes his lips, he is deemed intelligent" (Prov. 17:28). Abraham Lincoln, steeped in Scripture, would quip, "It is better to remain silent and seem a fool, than to speak and remove all doubt!"

To be slow to speak entails that we *think* before we speak, that we *listen* to others while they talk, rather than merely preparing our own response, and that we take time as well to listen to God speaking within us first so that the Holy Spirit can teach us what to say (see Luke 12:12). Such slowness of speech builds in us docility both to earthly teachers and to the Heavenly Teacher.

In regard to this first maxim, Thomas clearly practiced what he preached. Indeed, that is how he acquired his nickname "the Dumb Ox"! Thomas was barely out of his teens when he went to the University of Paris to study with his great mentor, St. Albert the Great, the quintessential German professor, who would go on to become the patron saint of scientists. Judging by Thomas's massive frame and very quiet demeanor, his fellow students assumed he was a not-very-bright country bumpkin, and they dubbed him the Dumb Ox. The most literal meaning of "dumb" is an inability or unwillingness to speak, and its secondary meaning, as you well know, is dull-wittedness. Well, one day, one of his more

---

[17] Sertillanges and Ryan, *The Intellectual Life*, 21.

considerate fellow students offered to "help" the young ox with a difficult lesson. The normally taciturn Thomas proceeded to explain the passage to him with a depth of understanding that made the student's jaw drop.

St. Albert, their master, had been aware of Thomas's prodigious mental powers all along. He informed his students that the "bellowing" of the Dumb Ox would one day be heard around the world. Brother John sought his bellowing in their day—and here we are, in all parts of the world, attentively listening to his wise bellowing nearly eight hundred years later!

Thomas gave one other piece of advice here, grown from his experience in religious community life. He warns Brother John not too readily to seek out the common gathering room if the purpose is merely to chat, distracting him from things that really matter. We might think of such common, chatting rooms in our own lives, be it the office water cooler, the gym's locker room, a local pub, or wherever it might be, and ask ourselves if we enter them too eagerly and too frequently, frittering time away that might be better spent in more important endeavors.

---

## Doctor's Orders

*Prescription for Taming Your*
*Tongue and Unleashing Your Mind*

### Reflect

Which lessons within this chapter struck a chord with you? Have you trained yourself in docility, becoming willing to learn from anyone who might possess knowledge or perspectives you may lack? Do you tend to speak first and think later, with perhaps at times unfortunate results? If so, can you work on slowing down just a bit and training your tongue to look before it leaps? Do you like to think and grow in knowledge but are too reticent to speak out and share what you have learned with others? A motto of St. Thomas's Dominican Order is "to share with others the fruits of contemplation," and Thomas himself would write: "For even as it is better to enlighten than merely to shine, so it is better to give to others the fruits of one's contemplation than merely to contemplate."[18] And, of course, the greatest Teacher of all advises us not to hide our lights under baskets or keep our talents buried under the ground (see Matt. 5:14–16; 25:14–30).

### Read

Wonderful insights on Thomas's letter on study can be found in Victor White's *Letter of St. Thomas to Brother John*, if you can track down a copy, (perhaps through interlibrary loan, as I did). First published in 1947, it is barely more than forty delightful pages long. Happily, far more readily available in multiple editions is A. D. Sertillanges's aforementioned masterpiece, *The Intellectual Life: Its Spirit, Conditions, Methods*. First published in French in 1920, this book is also inspired by Thomas's letter and contains more than 180 pages of elaborative insights. St. Thomas also writes specifically and briefly about docility as a part of the virtue of prudence in his *Summa Theologica*, II-II, Q. 49, art. 3. Among Thomas's other writings bearing on learning is his *De Magistro* (*On the Teacher*), as can be found in Mary Helen Mayer, M.A., ed., *The Philosophy of Teaching of St. Thomas Aquinas*.[19]

---

[18] *Summa Theologica*, II-II, Q. 188, art. 6.
[19] St. Thomas Aquinas, *De Magistro*, in *The Philosophy of Teaching of St. Thomas Aquinas*, ed. Mary Helen Mayer (Milwaukee, WI: Bruce, 1929).

## Remember

Thomas was a master of learning, of reasoning, and indeed of remembering, too (as we'll see in chapter 7). At this point in our journey upstream, I'll simply invite you to memorize the gist of the meaning (not the exact words—which were originally in Latin anyway!) of at least one of each chapter's lessons as we progress through the book. To give you a head start: chapter 1's title was "Speak Slowly and Carry a Big Heart and Mind."[20] It addressed this Thomistic precept: "Be slow to speak, and slow to enter the common room where people chat." To listen before you speak is certainly one key lesson worth remembering.

Got it? Good. Now let's continue our way upstream as St. Thomas reveals to us how maintaining a pure conscience and the habit of frequent prayer will lead us not only to knowledge, but to happiness and holiness, too.

---

[20] Yes, you are correct. It's a play on President Roosevelt's famous maxim, "Speak softly and carry a big stick." For our purposes, we forgo the stick and replace it with a loving heart and a mind that thirsts for truth.

*Chapter 2*

# The Power of Pure Prayer

*Hold fast to the purity of conscience. Do
not cease to make time for prayer.*

## How Purity of Heart Benefits the Mind

We study to seek truth, and Truth Himself declared to us, "Blessed
are the pure of heart, for they shall see God" (Matt. 5:8). Only
when our *heart*, our *conscience*, and our *will* are pure, free from the
distractions of temptation and the stains of sin, can our intellects
gaze clearly upon truth. Prudence is the virtue that guides the moral
virtues of temperance, fortitude, and justice, *but it also depends on
them*. It is through the exercise of virtues such as self-control and
courage that we can discipline our minds to focus on what is truly
important and then act to achieve it. Moral virtue strengthens
and sharpens our powers of understanding so that they may better "penetrate into the heart of things." We will not achieve the
heights of intellectual virtue, of knowing the true in the manner
of St. Thomas, without at the same time climbing and growing in
the moral virtue of striving to seek only what is truly good.

St. Thomas was well aware of how temptations toward sexual
impurity and other bodily sins can draw our hearts and minds
away from the things that matter most. In writing about the

"daughters" of the vice of *acedia* (or spiritual sloth) he declared, echoing the philosopher Aristotle, that "those who find no joy in spiritual pleasures have recourse to pleasures of the body."[21]

Indeed, when Thomas as a young man had dedicated his life to preaching and teaching Christ's gospel as a member of the new, humble Dominican Order, his biological brothers were so outraged that they captured him on the road to Paris and took him back to the family's castle. There, his brothers explicitly endeavored to remove his mind from spiritual things through a powerful temptation to bodily pleasure. They introduced a beautiful young courtesan into his room, whereupon Thomas brandished a log from the fireplace and chased her out the door, making a sign of the cross on the door with the firebrand when he slammed it shut behind her! Pious legend reports that angels then came to his aid and gave him a girdle of chastity, whereupon he was never again tempted by sensual bodily pleasures, as he immersed himself totally in the joys of the intellect and the spirit.

Of course, we all have different bodies, temperaments, and dispositions, and some of us, by nature, suffer greater temptations to impurity than others do. As a young man, St. Augustine famously prayed that God would give him chastity, "but not yet." St. Paul wrote of the war between the flesh and the spirit, and how easy it is for carnal, enfleshed human beings to leave undone the good things we want to do while doing the evil things that we hate (see Rom. 7:13–22), echoing Christ's warning to Peter that in matters of temptation, "the spirit indeed is willing but the flesh is weak" (Matt. 26:41).

---

[21] *Summa Theologica*, II-II, Q. 35, art. 4, citing Aristotle's *Nicomachean Ethics*, bk. 5, chap. 6.

Thomas has provided a rather abstract-sounding but exceedingly practical bit of advice that can go a long way toward helping the spirit conquer the flesh so that we can focus upon higher things: "Hence, the most effective remedy against intemperance is not to dwell on the consideration of singulars."[22]

Lust, the most powerful challenge to the virtue of temperance and purity of heart, thrives on singulars, especially visual images of particular enticing bodies. Unfortunately, advertisers and the purveyors of popular media know this so well that we are perpetually bombarded by images purposely designed to arouse our lusts, be it on television shows and commercials, in movies, in newspapers and magazines, or plastered greater than life-size on unavoidable roadside billboards. The styles of dress, attitudes, and manners of behavior they promote bear fruit in the attire and demeanor of real flesh-and-blood men and women. Males, by our nature, are especially prone to distraction by these images, both through the media and in daily life. What, then, are we to do?

St. Thomas suggests that we focus on the opposite of those "singulars" that we grasp with our senses as animals do; namely, we should turn our attention to the "universals" that only we humans can grasp through our God-given intellects. Instead of focusing on this or that particular woman, try focusing on "woman." Instead of focusing on, and perhaps lusting after, this particular woman, try focusing on her role as a daughter or a sister, and perhaps as someone else's current or future wife or mother. Instead of emulating the Don Juan–like "lover" who lusts after women (and does not really love them), why not emulate the man who shows true love

---

[22] *Summa Theologica*, II-II, Q. 142, art. 3.

for women by honoring and respecting them? Why not become more acquainted with Pope John Paul II's Theology of the Body to gain a beautifully profound understanding of the true wonder of the fact that God made us man and woman?

The couple blessed with the sacrament of marriage can treat each other with special loving attention as singulars, but they, too, must love rather than lust, loving each other in the flesh, yet never seeing or using the other as mere flesh alone. St. Thomas was especially adept at practicing temperance because of his focus on the very highest of universals, the divine things of God. Spiritual sloth, he wrote, paves the way for lust and intemperance, because he knew that "those who find no joy in spiritual things have recourse to pleasures of the body."[23] To curb lust, then, let us focus most on the highest things of God, from which flows love, not lust. The pure of heart, after all, will see God.

Regardless of the nature or intensity of our temptations, we also have access to the grace of God, the ultimate remedy for the bodily yearnings that pull us away from contemplation and spiritual joys. As Eastern Father St. John Climacus stated so well:

> Do not imagine that you will overwhelm the demon of fornication by entering into an argument with him. Nature is on his side and he has the best of the argument. So the man who decides to struggle against his flesh and to overcome it by his own efforts is fighting in vain. The truth is that unless the Lord overturns the house of the flesh and builds the house of the soul, the man wishing to overcome it has watched and fasted for nothing. Offer up to the Lord the weakness of your nature. Admit your

[23] Ibid., II-II, Q. 35, art. 4.

incapacity and, without your knowing it, you will win for yourself the gift of chastity.[24]

Of course, it is not only sins of lust that can lead to an impure conscience. If we are to think like Aquinas, we must strive against all manner of sin, to build all manner of virtue, and to ask God to help us in battle; we must also thank Him when we emerge victorious. In fact, this leads us to Thomas's next precept.

## *The Power of Prayer in Perfecting Our Thinking (and Doing)*

Prayer is the Christian's fundamental means of acquiring virtue: "If any of you lack wisdom, let him ask God, who gives to all men generously" (James 1:5). Indeed, St. Thomas, our great preacher and teacher, clearly practiced what he preached and taught, crediting his vast learning more to prayer than to study! Hear the words of Thomas's close friend, Brother Reginald of Piperno, quoted at Thomas's canonization proceedings: "When perplexed by a difficulty he would kneel and pray and then, on returning to his writing and dictation, he was accustomed to find that his thought had become so clear that it seemed to show him inwardly, as in a book, the words he needed."[25] Might we all develop such a prayerful practice to overcome writer's (or studier's) block!

Further, as Father White makes clear in this context: "In prayer only do we stand face to face with the Teacher, '*qui solus interius et principaliter docet*,' and without whose constant assistance

---

[24] St. John Climacus, *The Ladder of Divine Ascent* (New York: Paulist Press, 1982), 173.

[25] As cited in Mary Carruthers, *The Book of Memory: A Study of Memory in Medieval Culture* (New York: Cambridge University Press, 1990), 6.

and light we can learn nothing."[26] Only in prayer do we make direct contact with that ultimate Teacher and Maker of all Truths, and that is why it should undergird all our studies.

Father White cites a bit of the text from the *Summa Theologica*[27] in which Thomas notes that we reach truth in *two ways*. In the first way, we receive truth from outside ourselves, and to access such truths directly from God, *prayer* is our means. Indeed, he cites the words of Wisdom 7:7: "I called upon God, and the spirit of wisdom came upon me."[28] As far as gaining truths from other people, our means are *hearing* the spoken word and *reading* the Holy Scriptures. The second method in which we reach truth through our actions requires personal *study* and *meditation*.

Prayer then, is our God-given means of acquiring His wisdom. In expounding on the various acts of the virtue of religion, Thomas writes, "According to Cassiodorus, *prayer* (*oratio*) is *spoken reason* (*oris ratio*)."[29] Speech and reason are powers of the intellect, so prayer is not an act of the lower powers of sensation we share with other animals, but of our uniquely human intellectual powers.

Lower animals cannot pray. When Psalm 146:9 tells us that God gives food to the beasts and ravens that call upon Him, it refers to the natural, instinctual desire for God implanted in animals, and not to actual prayer.

God Himself does not pray because there is nothing He needs from another. Further, prayer is an act of reason that consists

---

[26] Aquinas and White, *How to Study*, 23.

[27] *Summa Theologica*, II-II, Q. 180, art. 3, ad. 4.

[28] In the RSVCE the full verse reads: "Therefore I prayed, and understanding was given me; I called upon God, and the spirit of wisdom came to me."

[29] *Summa Theologica*, II-II, Q. 83, art. 3.

in beseeching or requesting things from a superior. No being is above the Divine Persons of God.

Prayer, then, is the province of the rational animal, and that animal is man. Thomas notes that prayer starts with and is essentially "the raising up of one's mind to God."[30] Further, the "parts" of prayer include *supplications* (humble requests) and *thanksgiving* for blessings God has provided.

St. Thomas, the master philosopher and logician, was also quite the master of prayer. Indeed, he wrote the liturgy for the feast of Corpus Christi that Pope Urban V instituted in 1264. The beautiful, euphonious prayers that he crafted are still used at Masses today. They include such glorious prayerful hymns as the "Lauda Sion Salvatorem" (Sion, Lift Up Thy Voice and Sing), "Pange Lingua" (Sing, Tongue, the Mystery of the Glorious Body), "Tantum Ergo" (Down in Adoration Falling), and the sublime "Panis Angelicus" (Bread of Angels).[31]

Because Thomas knew well what Father Sertillanges has stated so elegantly—that "the light of God does not shine under your study lamp, unless your soul asks for it with persistent effort"[32]—he even crafted a special prayer that he recited before studying. Here is a brief excerpt:

> Ineffable Creator,
> Who, from the treasures of Your wisdom,

[30] Ibid., II-II, Q. 83, art. 17.

[31] We are blessed to have their recordings in many versions free online with but a few keystrokes, clicks of a mouse, or flicks of a finger. I encourage you to track down and enjoy them. Indeed, reading Thomas's insights while listening to his hymns at low volume can help us to think and to love God like Aquinas.

[32] Sertillanges and Ryan, *The Intellectual Life*, 15.

have established three hierarchies of angels,
have arrayed them in marvelous order
above the fiery heavens,
and have marshaled the regions
of the universe with such artful skill ...
grant to me keenness of mind,
capacity to remember,
skill in learning,
subtlety to interpret,
and eloquence of speech.
May You guide the beginning of my work,
direct its progress, and bring it to completion.[33]

The lesson could not be clearer: if we are to *think* like Aquinas, then we must *pray* like him, too![34]

---

### Doctor's Orders

*Prescription for Building a Pure Conscience
and a Powerful Prayer Life*

#### Reflect

Which of Thomas's lessons in this chapter most hit you? Do you see the need to purify your conscience, to rein in your passions and desires, to focus more clearly on learning God's will and

---

[33] *The Aquinas Prayer Book: The Prayers and Hymns of St. Thomas Aquinas*, ed. Robert Anderson and Johann Moser (Manchester, NH: Sophia Institute Press, 2000), 43.

[34] Not necessarily in Thomas's own words, but as an ingrained habit, striving for the same kind of intense love, thoughtful devotion, and heartfelt gratitude toward God.

guiding your life by His loving counsel? Do you see how prayer can help us achieve purity of conscience and help perfect our intellectual powers by opening our minds to God's illumination? If you do not have a regular habit of prayer, how can you rearrange your schedule to add at least a few minutes for prayer every day, first thing in the morning, last thing at night, ideally at many brief moments throughout the day, and, lest I forget, before every time you sit down to study?

**Read**

Thomas wrote extensively about the virtue of temperance that reins in our passions.[35] Regarding the subject of prayer, we are also very much blessed by Thomas and the Thomists. Thomas addresses the subject of prayer in a full seventeen articles of his *Summa*, II-II, Q. 83. *The Aquinas Prayer Book* includes many of Thomas's wonderful prayers in the amazingly rhymed original Latin on the left-hand pages with elegant English translations on the right. Thomas also preached wonderful sermons, commenting line by line on the Apostles' Creed, the Our Father, and the Hail Mary, which can be found in *The Aquinas Catechism*.[36] I can also highly recommend *Aquinas at Prayer: The Bible, Mysticism, and Poetry* by Paul Murray, O.P.[37] Indeed, Murray argues that because of the beautiful prayers he crafted, Thomas, our *thinker* extraordinaire, was also the greatest Latin *poet* of the Middle Ages (and I'm inclined to agree with him!).

---

[35] In Aquinas, *Summa Theologica*, II-II, Q. 141-70.
[36] *The Aquinas Catechism: A Simple Explanation of the Catholic Faith by the Church's Greatest Theologian* (Manchester, NH: Sophia Institute Press, 2000).
[37] Paul Murray, *Aquinas at Prayer: The Bible, Mysticism and Poetry* (London: Bloomsbury Continuum, 2013).

**Remember**

I invite you to try to remember this chapter's title or the gist of Thomas's recommendation for striving for a pure conscience. And if I might suggest one more thing worth remembering, consider praying Thomas's prayer before study every time you sit down to study until you can pray it from memory.

*Chapter 3*

# From the Cell to the Wine Cellar:
# On Crafting a Study Space You Can Love

*Love to frequently be in your cell, if you wish
to be admitted to the wine cellar.*

## The Chambers of the King

Wine lovers take note that while Thomas surely saw wine as
a good thing in moderation—echoing, in the *Summa Theologica*, Sirach 31:27: "Wine is like life to men, if you drink it in
moderation"[38]—he is speaking here to Brother John in a metaphorical sense; the wine cellar recalls the words not of Sirach but
of King Solomon, where he speaks of the chambers of the king,
the place where God calls us to dwell with Him.[39]

Thomas's advice is a call to *the love of solitude*, the capacity
to embrace and enjoy being alone with none but God for the
spiritual and intellectual benefits such intimate companionship
brings. In simplicity and silence we prepare ourselves to hear

[38] *Summa Theologica*, II-II, Q. 150, art. 1.
[39] Song of Sol. 1:4. In the Latin Vulgate Bible that St. Thomas
used, Solomon's Canticle of Canticles 1:3 uses the word *cellaria*
for cellars or storerooms.

the voice of God and to focus our intellects upon whatever task He has laid before us. We might ask ourselves if our study room is more like a monastic cell of solitude or a vibrating, pulsating, electronic entertainment center besieging us with sundry sounds and images that draw our minds anywhere but toward the king's chambers. If it is more like the latter, I feel confident that St. Thomas would advise us to shut unneeded, distracting things off during times dedicated to study and prayer.[40]

Further, we will be wise to equip our study spaces with whatever we will need when it comes time to study: our computer, books, writing materials, and perhaps a glass of water (or, better yet, a nice mug of stout coffee!). Of course, we are not always able to study in our favorite study place. We need to organize our minds as well, so that we might still be able to study with

[40] Cf. Sertillanges and Ryan, *The Intellectual Life*, 168–169. The good Father Sertillanges makes a case for what might be an exception to silence in solitude at times: "Who does not know that in listening to music an intellectual may get an impression of greatness, beauty, and power which is immediately transposed into his ordinary modes of thinking, furthers his purposes, colors his customary themes, and will presently enrich his work?... Music has this precious quality for the intellectual that as it conveys no precise ideas, it interferes with none. It awakens states of soul, from which each one in his particular task will draw what he will." (Admittedly, Father Sertillanges was not referring explicitly to listening to music *while* studying. He wrote long before the day of CDs and computers. I will still use it to justify my playing classical music or Gregorian chant softly as I study and write. In fact, let me check right now. Okay, currently playing is Haydn's sprightly Symphony No. 23 in G. No wonder I'm enjoying this session in my cell! My favorite pieces of soft background music for studying and writing, by the way, are the symphonies and Masses of Anton Bruckner. Check them out someday and enjoy!)

profit while we wait for our flight to board, or perhaps for a root canal.

Thomas himself was renowned for his amazing powers of concentration regardless of his setting. He would become so mentally focused at times that he'd become unaware of his surroundings—the ultimate absentminded professor. In one famous incident, lost in thought among other guests at the dinner table of St. Louis, king of France, Thomas smashed his mighty mitt upon the table and bellowed out, "And *that* will settle the Manicheans!" (He had been busy contemplating the answer to their philosophical and theological errors while those around him were contemplating small talk and appetizers.) Thomas had developed the power to carry his study cell with him wherever he went—even into the literal chambers of the king!

If we modernize and laicize Thomas's language of the monk's or friar's *cell* to the modern layperson's *study*, we will see that the virtue that he so thoroughly mastered could not be more at home in it. So, let's begin our study of this virtue most at home in the study.

### Curiositas Killed the Cat; Studiositas Brought It Back

It is within his consideration of temperance, the virtue of self-restraint, that Thomas reveals that *studiositas* (studiousness) is a related virtue in its own right. He provides a fascinating contrast between the virtue of studiousness and its contrary vice of *curiositas* (curiosity). Studiousness moderates the natural human desire to know[41]—for there is much in this world that is not worth knowing, that feeds our baser desires and diverts us from higher things.

---

[41] Thomas quite agreed with the opening line of Aristotle's *Metaphysics* that "all men by their nature desire to know."

The vice of curiosity is the desire to know and pry into things that we should leave alone. It creates and then feeds upon boredom and inattentiveness. Just look at that guy with the television remote control, clicking away again and again and again. Hey, that's not *you*, is it? (Or perhaps I've just seen *my* reflection in the screen.)

Studiousness, on the other hand, is the virtue whereby we seek not fleeting entertainments but lasting wisdom, as Scripture advises: "Study wisdom, my son, and make my heart joyful, that thou mayest give an answer to him that reproaches."[42]

Thomas defines "study" as "the keen application of the mind to something." He adds: "Now the mind is not applied to a thing except by knowing a thing."[43] *Studiousness* regulates our desire to study and know. Studiousness has a restraining function when it holds back our *natural intellectual desires* to know things that are not worth knowing and that lead to distraction and possibly sin. Studiousness has a positive, motivating function when it overcomes our *natural bodily resistance* to the attention and diligence prolonged study can require. As with any natural virtue, we build it by practicing it, by reining in idle curiosity, and by hitting the books when we might feel like hitting the computer or the mattress instead.

Every serious thinker, before patting himself on the back for his shining virtue of studiousness, should be aware that under several conditions even the study of intellectual truths can resemble the vice of curiosity more than the virtue of studiousness. Thomas notes that study can be sinful if it is driven by pride—by

---

[42] Prov. 27:11, as cited in Aquinas, *Summa Theologica*, II-II, Q. 166, art. 1.
[43] *Summa Theologica*, II-II, Q. 166, art. 1.

the desire to appear knowledgeable rather than by the desire for truth. Study can also be sinful if one seeks out knowledge in order to commit evil acts. (This might call to mind the cruel medical experiments of Nazi physicians, for example.)

Further, Thomas notes four ways in which study can be sinful because the subject matter we study is "inordinate":

1. When a person is drawn away from an important topic he is obliged to study by a less profitable study. Thomas gives an example from St. Jerome of priests forsaking study of the Gospels and the prophets to overindulge in reading stage plays or singing popular love songs. A common example in our day would be students absorbed in reading their e-mail on their phones during their teacher's lecture. (I hope that my surgeon did not have such study habits while in medical school!)

2. When one seeks to learn from people "by whom it is unlawful to be taught."[44] Thomas provides examples of people who sought to know the future through consulting with demons. This is called "superstitious curiosity," and we see it today in those drawn to the occult.

3. When people desire to know the truth about creatures while ignoring knowledge about their Creator. We see this in some scientists who ignore or deny that the organisms or phenomena they study are *creatures*, which implies *creation* and requires a *Creator*. Indeed, St. Paul wrote millennia earlier that "ever since the creation of the world his invisible nature, namely his eternal power and deity, has been clearly perceived in

---

[44] Ibid., II-II, Q. 167, art. 1.

the things that have been made" (Rom. 1:20). Thomas's teacher St. Albert, realizing this truth, would write that "the whole world is theology for us because the heavens proclaim the glory of God."[45] Thomas himself, awed by the implications of this, would write of God: "He produced many and diverse creatures, that what was wanting to one in the representation of the divine goodness, which in God is simple and uniform, in creatures is manifold and divided; and hence the whole universe together participates in the divine goodness more perfectly, and represents it better than any single creature whatever."[46] We might well ask if we have trained ourselves to see traces of God's beauty and goodness in the myriad of creatures in the world around us.

4. When a person studies to know the truth above the capacity of his intelligence. Might this ring any bells? "Seek not the things that are too high for you," said Sirach (3:21) and St. Thomas in his letter on study. Here again, we must study within the limits of our abilities, bearing in mind and thanking God that, as our knowledge base grows, so too will our capacity to reach truths that rise progressively higher.

The virtue of studiousness, then, reins in our desire to study the wrong things for the wrong reasons and fires our desire to learn the highest, most important things of God within our

---

[45] From St. Albert's *Commentary on St. Matthew*, as cited in Paul Murray, *The New Wine of Dominican Spirituality: A Drink Called Happiness* (New York: Burns and Oates, 2006), 93. See Psalm 19 (18):1.

[46] *Summa Theologica*, I, Q. 47, art. 1.

capacity, in a virtuous circle that increases both our desire and our capacity to know the things that matter the most.

Happily for us, the exercise of any virtue brings with it the wholesome pleasure that comes from perfecting and utilizing the powers God has given us. When we have trained ourselves to yield less often to both the fleeting distractions of *curiosity* and the sloth of intellectual laziness, the virtue of *studiousness* will bring pleasures of its own, so that we will come to enjoy being frequently in our earthly study cells as we wait to spend eternity learning the glories of the universe from its Maker in His heavenly chambers.

---

## Doctor's Orders ✍

*Prescription for Three More Rs to Study in Your Study*

### Reflect

What lessons did you glean from this chapter? Could your study "cell" use a little remodeling? Might you train yourself to turn off potential distractions, such as e-mail, your cell phone, or the TV, while you devote time to study? If you feel the need to check e-mail, surf the Web, and so forth before you get down to business, have you considered setting a time limit (you can use a timer) so that your time will not be frittered away? Do you need to organize your desk and shelves so you have what you need when you need it? Could you try to grow in your appreciation of periods of silent solitude, or perhaps soft, muted instrumental or chanted background music while you study? Have you considered how to make more conducive to study the places where you have to sit and wait? Are you going to be stuck at an airport with hours of idle time between flights, or perhaps in a doctor's or a dentist's waiting room? Consider sitting far from the noisy television sets, and rather than picking up a celebrity magazine, bring along a worthwhile book to dig into. You never know what surprising goods might come from it. Indeed, I once made a new doctor/Catholic author friend that way![47]

## Read

Speaking again of reading, and now of reading recommendations, let's emphasize again that the act of *reading* itself can be an exercise in the virtue of studiousness, and again, how just *carrying* a book can sometimes produce interesting results! Just last week at an airport in Dallas, I noticed a trim, muscular African American waiter, who I guessed to be in his 30s or 40s, efficiently attending to all his customers. He was not my waiter, but he came over to tell me how pleased he was to see that I had a fairly hefty biography sitting on my table.[48] He told me that

---

[47] In 2015, while attending an appointment with my wife, I noticed that her doctor kept glancing at a book I had with me. He asked what it was, and I told him it was a biography of Blessed Jordan of Saxony, St. Dominic's successor at the helm of the Order of Preachers, and that I was working on a book on Dominican saints. The doctor beamed a great smile as he told us that he was Catholic, too, and had just written a work of fiction about doctors who cherished life in a futuristic world in which the Hippocratic oath upholding life had been replaced by the "Kevorkian" oath, inspired by the twentieth-century American champion of "physician-assisted suicide," Jack Kevorkian, also known as "Doctor Death." Indeed, we got so carried away with author-to-author banter that we *almost* left the office without getting a prescription for my wife!

[48] For those who might care to know, it happened to be Harlow Giles Unger's *Lafayette*. Oh, and my doctor friend's book is *The Kevorkian Oath* by Richard E. Brown, M.D.

he observes thousands of people a year as they eat or wait for their planes, and he sees fewer and fewer people with books, as more and more travelers sit immersed in the flittering worlds of their cell phones or the airport's ubiquitous television screens. He noted what a wonderful thing it is to be able to enter into and linger in the worlds that good books bring us, and he said he makes it a point to talk to every book reader he sees in the restaurant! I thanked this thoughtful, studious gentleman for his comments and assured him I could not agree more. This man knew the value of the virtue of studiousness. If you would care to read more about studiousness itself, as well as its nemesis, curiosity, I direct you to Thomas's *Summa Theologica*, II-II, questions 166 and 167.

### Remember

Do you remember our chapter's title and its key themes? And, just out of curiosity (if you'll forgive me), I wonder if you can recall at this point the key themes of our previous chapters. Got them? Great! If you don't have them, don't fret. St. Thomas has also given us wonderful guidelines to perfect powers of memory. We'll examine them in chapter 7 and then use them throughout the remainder of this book.

*Chapter 4*

# The Benefits and Perils of Friendliness to Study

*Show yourself amiable to everybody, or at least try; but become overly familiar with no one, for familiarity breeds contempt and introduces complications that will impede study.*

## *On the Friendliness That Is Called Affability*[49]

Thomas explains in his other writings that amiability, affability, or simply put, friendliness, is a part of the virtue of justice, something we owe to every person we meet.[50] Such fraternal charity also helps promote the kind of peace and goodwill that are most conducive to study. Brother John would not likely study so well if he fueled animosity and murmuring among his brethren, and neither will we study very well if we've aggrieved those with whom we live and study, be they fellow students or family members. Still, recognizing always that moral virtues generally involve a *golden mean*, a just right balance between too much

---

[49] This is Thomas's title for question 114 in his *Summa Theologica*, II-II.

[50] Ibid., building on Sirach 4:7: "Make yourself beloved in the congregation."

and too little of a good thing, Thomas warns against an excess of friendliness that may complicate study by drawing our attention to trivial interpersonal issues and that may stir animosity toward us if our attentions to another are overbearing and bring to light our weaknesses. Thomas warns of two vices contrary to friendliness: the vice of excess, called *flattery*, and the vice of deficiency, called *quarreling*.

As for flattery, Thomas cites an intriguing medieval gloss[51] on Ezekiel 13:18 of the Vulgate. It appears as follows in the *Summa Theologica*: "Woe to them that sew cushions under every elbow." Thomas notes that the gloss says, "*That is to say, sweet flattery. Therefore, flattery is a sin.*"[52] Thomas explains that when we exercise the virtue of friendliness, we seek to bring pleasure to those with whom we work and live, but we do not hesitate to bring displeasure to another when our affability would encourage another person in some evil intention or condone an evil act. Indeed, one of the traditional seven spiritual acts of mercy, each of which Thomas describes as "a charity through the medium of mercy,"[53] is to "reprove the sinner."[54] We sometimes display our friendliness when we explain our disapproval of a companion's statement or

---

[51] The *Glossa Ordinaria*, widely used in the Middle Ages, was a version of the Latin Vulgate Bible that contained, in the margins of the text, brief glosses (comments or explanations) that were compiled from the writings of various Church Fathers. Thomas availed himself of this gloss regularly and would later compile his own truly remarkable *Catena Aurea* (*Golden Chain*) of commentary on all four Gospels, featuring the line-by-line comments of more than eighty Eastern and Western Church Fathers, often with three or four Fathers' comments on each set of verses.

[52] *Summa Theologica*, II-II, Q. 115, art. 1.

[53] Ibid., II-II, Q. 32, art. 1.

[54] Ibid., II-II, Q. 32, art. 2.

act for his own good. The flatterer praises companions regardless of what they say or do, "sewing cushions under every elbow" to comfort and to please, but to his friend's and his own detriment.

In describing the vice of deficient friendliness, called quarreling, Thomas notes that, while the friendly person generally hopes and strives to *please* others, the quarrelsome person derives pleasure from *displeasing* others. The quarrelsome person finds it agreeable to disagree and takes joy in contradicting those around him. Thomas approvingly cites Aristotle, who wrote in his *Nicomachean Ethics*, book 4, chapter 6, that "those who are opposed to everything with the intent of being disagreeable, and care for nobody, are said to be peevish and quarrelsome."[55] These people are "aginners": they don't care what you argue for; they are going to speak out "agin" it!

Surely, we can see the simple practicality of this bit of advice to Brother John. When it comes to enhancing our capacity to study, flattery will get us nowhere, and quarreling will stir resentments and passions unsuited to the peace and tranquility that facilitate study. Either kind of familiarity is bound to breed contempt and interfere with study.

Though Thomas was studious and prone to deep contemplation by his natural disposition, he built upon nature with self-discipline and training and perfected it through his openness of God's grace. Though perhaps at his best and most fulfilled in the realm of solitude, study, and prayer, Thomas felt that his highest calling was to share the truths he had gleaned with his neighbors, including the friars he lived with, the students he taught, and, in the broadest sense, those of us who read him today, and who will read him, God willing, until kingdom come!

[55] Ibid., II-II, Q. 166, art. 1.

Further, the cerebral, self-sufficient Thomas did indeed practice the affability that he preached. One touching and amusing
story relates that a young friar arrived at the Dominican convent
in Paris for the first time and wanted to see its wonderful sights.
A prior advised him to ask one of the religious there to give him
a tour of the city. The first man the young friar chanced upon
was a quite large, placid-looking man. He told the man that the
prior said he had to show him around. The large friar complied
for the next few hours, without a word of complaint, even when
his young companion chided him at times for moving too slowly
to suit him. We can imagine that young friar's reaction when
he later found out from others that the humble tour guide he
had pressed into service was the world's foremost professor and
theologian, Thomas Aquinas!

### Ora et Labora — et Ludo!

*Ora et labora*, "pray and work," is a classic Benedictine motto
that our great Dominican scholar knew and practiced well. He
also knew the wisdom of the later aphorism that "all work and
no play makes Jack a dull boy," and that is where *ludo* comes in
to play, since *ludo* is Latin for "play." Thomas addressed the value
and the virtues of play and playfulness in the *Summa Theologica*.

Hear Thomas, for example, on the value of playful games,
even for the scholar in pursuit of knowledge and holiness (indeed, even for a saint loved by Christ):

> Just as weariness of the body is dispelled by resting the
> body, so weariness of the soul needs be remedied by resting
> the soul; and the soul's rest is pleasure.... Now suchlike
> words or deeds wherein nothing further is sought than the
> soul's delight, are called playful or humorous. Hence it is

necessary at times to make use of them, in order to give rest, as it were, to the soul.[56]

And how does the saint loved by Christ figure in? Well, between our ellipsis in the paragraph above, Thomas relates a delightful story from St. John Cassian's book *Conferences of the Fathers*, about Christ's "beloved disciple," St. John the Evangelist. A group of observers was scandalized when they saw St. John playing with some of his disciples. (How intriguing a scene! Don't you wish you were there to see it?) John saw that one man in that easily scandalized troop was carrying a bow and arrow. He asked the man to shoot an arrow into the air, and several more after that. He then asked the man if he could keep shooting them indefinitely. The man replied that he could not, because if he continued to do so, the bow would eventually break. Thomas concludes the little story as follows: "Whence the Blessed John drew the inference that in a like manner man's mind would break if its tension were never relaxed!"[57]

Thomas, like St. John Cassian before him, and St. John the Evangelist before both of them, clearly saw the value of some good, clean fun, in moderation, of course. Indeed, in his next article in the *Summa*, Thomas does warn of the harm and sinfulness of excessive play, and of jesting that is rude, scandalous, or obscene. In his final article on the topic, though, he explicitly encourages us to be mirthful with our companions: "In human affairs, whatever is against reason is a sin. Now, it is against reason for a man to be burdensome to others, by offering no pleasure to others, and by hindering their enjoyment."[58] Indeed, as a

---

[56] Ibid., II-II, Q. 168, art. 2.
[57] Ibid. (Exclamation point added!)
[58] Ibid., II-II, Q. 168, art. 4.

champion of "moderate mirth,"[59] Thomas would advise lovers of knowledge not to be buffoons incapable of seriousness, but neither would he advise us to be party poopers! Work, pray — and, sometimes, play!

### From Friendliness to Friendship

I would venture that most of you reading this book are not like Brother John. You are not friars, monks, canons, sisters, or nuns living together in a cloister (though I certainly hope and pray that some of you are!). My point is that regardless of our state of life and living situation, we should *all* be friendly toward *all* the people with whom we live and study.

We are also especially blessed if we have the opportunity to form *particular friendships*, intimate bonds with one or a few friends, whom we may come to treat as "a second self" and consider their happiness to be as important as our own. Thomas knew quite well Aristotle's discussion of a class of friendships based on the provision of mutual *pleasures*, a second based on *utility*, or the practical use friends can be of to one another, and a third, highest, truest form of friendship, based on each friend's *virtue* and serving to heighten the virtue of each. And far beyond even "the Philosopher's"[60] insights, Thomas knew that Christ came to earth so that He would no longer call us "servants," but "friends."[61] Indeed, Thomas's magnificent treatise on the ultimate God-given virtue of charity is based on the principle that "charity is the friendship of man for God."[62]

---

[59] Ibid.
[60] Thomas's honorific title for Aristotle.
[61] *Summa Theologica*, II-II, Q. 23, art. 1, citing John 15:15.
[62] Ibid., II-II, Q. 23, art. 1.

With our focus on study and thinking, an overview of all of Thomas's insights on charity and friendship would take us way too far up a different stream, but I'll conclude with just one more Thomistic insight on friendship and virtuous works (such as study):

> [Aristotle] draws a conclusion concerning the good, that friendship between virtuous men is good and is always increased in goodness by exemplary conversation. Friends become better by working together and loving each other. For one receives from the other an example of virtuous work which is at the same time pleasing to him. Hence it is proverbial that man adopts noble deeds from noble men.[63]

Certainly among the world's most notable examples of virtuous friends spurring each other on toward the loftiest heights of virtue and the noblest deeds of study was that holy friendship between mentor and student, between the Church's "Universal Doctor" and her "Angelic Doctor," between the patron saint of scientists and the patron saint of scholars. I refer, of course, to the earthly friendship between St. Albert the Great and St. Thomas Aquinas. (Can we even begin to imagine the sublimity of their friendly conversations in heaven?)

In sum, then, we should be friendly to all, but not overly familiar, and should be watchful for a few virtuous friends with whom, through fruitful conversations and noble deeds, we might pull our oars in unison and row more strongly together up the stream toward ever deeper seas of knowledge and truth.

---

[63] *Commentary on the Nicomachean Ethics*, 87.

---

## Doctor's Orders ✍🏻

*Prescription for Finding the Right Balance
between Friendliness and Studiousness*

### Reflect

Have you been friendly enough, or perhaps too friendly with others before or while you need to get down to business and study? If you are a student, have you shunned an invitation to a study group that might be of help to you or to your fellow students? If you've joined such a group, do you help rein in the gossip and small talk so you can spur each other on to greater learning? Do you cultivate virtuous friendships and talk with your friends about noble things, such as how to grow wiser and holier?

### Read

St. Thomas addresses the virtue of friendliness we owe to everyone in question 114 of his *Summa Theologica*, II-II. He treats of the value of humor and play in question 168. His masterful exposition of charity as friendship with God begins with question 23, article 1. I'll note as well that I've written about Thomas's treatment of friendship in relation to the writings on friendship of Aristotle, Cicero, and the Cistercian abbot St. Aelred of Rievaulx.[64]

---

[64] In chapter 6, "Lightening the Load of Your Neighbor's Loneliness," of my book *The Catholic Guide to Loneliness: How Science and Faith Can Help Us Understand It, Grow from It, and Conquer It* (Sophia Institute Press, 2017). See also my book *The Four Friendships: From Aristotle to Aquinas* (Angelico Press, 2018).

### Remember

Do you remember the gist or key lessons of our first four precepts? To give you a brief refresher on some of the key themes, we've looked at the value of being quick to listen and slow to speak, of purity of conscience and the power of prayer, of learning to enjoy your place of study, and now, of keeping friendliness, fun, and friendship in the happy kind of balance that will maximize your pursuit of the truth.

*Chapter 5*

# Set Your Intellect Free by Avoiding Worldly Entanglements

*Also, do not get enmeshed in the words and deeds of worldly people. Above all, flee from aimless conversations.*

## The Perils of a World Growing Ever More Worldly

Thomas warns particularly about getting entangled in the words, deeds, and conversations of worldly people whose thoughts are not focused on the highest things of God. Drawing another insight from Aristotle's discussion of classes of friendships—those based on mutual *pleasures, utility,* and *virtue*—Thomas also knew well that Aristotle had declared that *virtuous friendships are rare because virtue is rare.*

Worldliness, unfortunately, is anything but rare, and most friendships never rise higher than a concern for the pleasures or other benefits one friend might gain from another.

Virtuous friendships are to be formed not with the worldly (unless they are willing to strive toward higher things), but with those who set their sights on God. Both common sense and modern psychology tell us how susceptible we are to the influences of our environment. Those who strive to think like Aquinas would be wise to exercise their free will to place themselves in the right environments, such as inside our cells of study and within the circle of virtuous, studious friends whom we have gathered around us. In such virtuous environs, conversations will be far from aimless. They'll aim squarely and surely at the true, the good, and the beautiful things of God.

Unfortunately, avoiding enmeshment in the words and deeds of worldly people may be more difficult in our day than in the days of Thomas and Brother John. Of this we can be certain: there are many new, compelling means to draw our minds from the higher things of God and enmesh them in worldly concerns. I speak of our modern electronic technologies of communication and entertainment.

Perhaps you have at times felt distracted by or even enmeshed in those virtual worlds on your desktop, on your lap, in the palm of your hand, or even plugged into your ear. Our modern electronic marvels can be incredible boons to the acquisition and sharing of knowledge. Having written all my college and graduate-level papers on an old-fashioned typewriter, and my master's thesis on a then (1990) modern marvel with a word-processing display of *one line* of visible text, I can hardly fathom how I could have completed my doctoral program and dissertation and proceeded to write a fair number of books without the aid of modern computers and their word-processing programs. Further, as I'm sure you can also attest, they prove invaluable not only for writing but for research and fact-checking, too. I am also quite thankful that through the wonder of cell-phone technology, I find myself talking, texting, and learning from people all over the world. Praise be to God!

And yet these wonderful tools are also exceptionally sharp two-edged swords. If they are not wielded with care, they can slice through our attempts to rein in our minds for serious study.

## Enmeshed, Scattered, and Hijacked Minds

Thomas wrote of the perils of enmeshment in worldliness in the middle of the thirteenth century. Here in the early twenty-first century, many voices are warning us of the novel tools of worldly entanglement; indeed, they may even entangle, or at least re-shape, the connections between our brain cells! In his book *The Shallows: What the Internet Is Doing to Our Brains* (W. W. Norton, 2010), Nicholas Carr, a modern writer on technology and culture, argues that by repeatedly practicing the sweeping, but fleeting and superficial scanning of information that electronic formats on the Internet supply, we are actually producing changes in our brain tissues and organization that make prolonged, sustained attention more difficult. Of course, it is hard to think deeply about things that you can't focus on!

In the very first line of his recent article, "How Smartphones Hijack Our Minds," Carr writes: "If you are like the typical owner, you'll be pulling your phone out and using it some 80 times a day, according to data that Apple collects."[65] He notes that this amounts to nearly 30,000 times in the course of the year. We would do well to ask ourselves if *we* are "typical owners," and if so, how this might square with St. Thomas's recommendation not to become "enmeshed" in the things of the world if we are to attain truth.

Such checking behaviors can become increasingly addictive and time-consuming because they operate on the principle that behavioral psychologists have termed "intermittent positive re-inforcement." We are more likely to perform repetitive behaviors more often when they are rewarded only at times, and when we

---

[65] Nicholas Carr, "How Smartphones Hijack Our Minds," *Wall Street Journal*, October 6, 2017.

don't know in advance which repetition will yield the reward. One of the simplest, most striking examples of intermittent reinforcement is seen in the payout ratios built into slot machines used for gambling. The gambler wins only once in a while and never knows whether the *very next pull* of the arm (or push of the button these days) is not the one that could bring home the jackpot. Of course, such gambling machines would generate no profits if people, on average, won more than they lost.

Well, our cell-phone or e-mail checking behaviors operate on just the same principle. Most of those eighty checks of the cell phone each day are not going to reveal some important message. Sometimes there will be nothing at all, or perhaps a bunch of junk mail. Yet, each time we check, our attention may be diverted from higher things, such as reading, study, prayer, or even simply paying attention to the people around us or the God-given beauties of nature. The good things of relationships and natural beauty are also there waiting for us—unless we've let little devices hijack our brains and drive them toward pettier things.

Speaking of cell phones, didn't Thomas advise us as well to "flee from aimless conversations"? (Hmm. Did the Angelic Doctor foresee those electronic hijackers more than seven centuries in advance?) What Thomas had in mind in his time was face-to-face conversation, and while we might bemoan their relative decrease, courtesy of technology, even face-to-face conservations should be curtailed if their content is not wholesome and doesn't lead us to higher things. Thomas warns, in the original Latin, against *discursus*: aimless wandering or meandering.

Those who would think like Aquinas will be affable to others and will engage in pleasantries and small talk at times. (Did I tell you, by the way, that we had snow here in April this year?) Indeed, a conversation can have a focused, worthwhile aim, even if it be merely to grease the wheel of polite social interactions. Those who would think like Aquinas will find no time, though, for inappropriate conversations, obscene language, malicious gossip or slander, or flattery or quarreling, as we saw in our last chapter. Those who would think like Aquinas will seek out time for study, though, and for conversations with higher-than-worldly aims, such as the truth, beauty, and goodness of God and Creation.

One of the most famous incidents in Thomas's life illustrates how he would engage in friendly conversation, but with a mind toward heavenly things. It occurred on the road to Paris. As Thomas and some fellow Dominican friars approached the great city, a brother friar stated how grand it would be to possess all of Paris's vast wealth. St. Thomas replied that he would rather have a copy of St. John Chrysostom's *Homilies on the Gospel of St. Matthew*![66]

---

## Doctor's Orders ✍

*Prescription for Getting Your Brain,*
*Mind, and Soul Disentangled*

### Reflect

Which take-home messages has Thomas wrapped up for you in this chapter? Have you allowed your mind to become hijacked or your soul entangled by things of the world? How many times

---

[66] As for the positive blessings of technology, I should note that Chrysostom's homilies, considered so invaluable by St. Thomas, are now free to all online! See, for example, New Advent, http://www.newadvent.org/fathers/2001.htm.

per day do you check your text messages, e-mails, or social media accounts? Even if, praise God, you connect most often with virtuous people, is all that checking really raising your mind toward higher things and strengthening intimate interpersonal bonds, or is it pulling you away from people and matters that matter much more? Further, are you allowing the one-way conversations of other media, such as the programming and advertisements of television, radio, the Internet, or even highway billboards to draw your mind and soul too often not only away from lofty things but to the pursuit of worldly pleasures and material things? These are questions well worth thinking about and acting upon.

## Read

For a modern look at the effects of too much worldly electronic stimulation upon the mind, and indeed, upon the brain that serves it, I highly recommend Nicholas Carr's aforementioned book, *The Shallows*. For an excellent Catholic perspective addressing the effects on the soul as well, see Christopher Blum and Joshua Hochschild's *A Mind at Peace: Reclaiming an Ordered Soul in the Age of Distraction* (Sophia Institute Press, 2017). I recommend again that you read, if you haven't done so, Thomas's writings on the virtue of *studiositas* and the vice of *curiositas* (*Summa Theologica*, II-II, Qs. 166 and 167) in light of the lenses provided in this chapter. And finally, come to think of it, why not dip into those homilies of St. John Chrysostom so cherished by St. Thomas? I've just done so for the first time. Deciding to see what he had to say about Christ's Sermon on the Mount, I jumped in at Homily 15. Commenting on the very first verses of that sermon (Matt. 5:1–2), St. John Chrysostom, in describing Christ's teaching methods, hits upon themes central to this book's focus on study and indeed central to this very chapter.

There he describes the need to become disentangled from the world, separating ourselves "from the tumults of ordinary life":

> [Jesus] sits in one spot: and that not in the midst of any city or forum, but on a mountain and in a wilderness; instructing us to do nothing for display, and to separate ourselves from the tumults of ordinary life, and this most especially, when we are to study wisdom, and to discourse of things needful to be done.[67]

### Remember

Do you recall our chapter's themes? The precept itself read: "Also, do not get enmeshed in the words and deeds of worldly people. Above all, flee from aimless conversations." And come to think of it, how are you doing with retaining the gist of the lessons of chapters 1 through 4? If you've got them—great! If not, we'll see if the lessons Thomas teaches to perfect our memories in chapter 7 make the task quite a bit more doable (and a lot more fun).

---

[67] Homily 15 in St. John Chrysostom, *Homilies on Matthew*, New Advent, http://www.newadvent.org/fathers/200115.htm.

*Chapter 6*

# The Imitation of Christ (and of Those Who Imitate Him)

*Do not fail to imitate the lives of saintly and noble men.*

## So Many Saints So Worthy of Our Imitation

What a great boon we all have in our heavenly extended family, the glorious communion of saints God has given us, through their willingness to devote themselves to Him. Not every saint is an intellectual or a scholar, but every saint knows how to center his life on the things that matter the most and therefore can share valuable lessons that every one of us should learn. With their Christ-centered heroic virtue, the saints can inspire and teach us all. The awesome self-discipline so many saints manifested and the external trials they endured should put into proper perspective the minor inconveniences and self-deprivations we undergo to pursue learning.

Perhaps it goes without saying that among the most noble and saintly of men we should strive to imitate is St. Thomas Aquinas, who, in his imitation of Christ, so devoutly exercised the great gifts God gave him. (In fact, that's why I'm writing and you're reading this book!) Thomas was a member of St. Dominic's Order of Preachers, the order with the motto of *Veritas* (Truth), the order upheld by study itself as one of its four pillars (the others being prayer, community, and preaching). The Dominican charism, with its intellectual bent, has been closest to my heart and mind since I was taught in grade school by wonderful Dominican Sisters. Still, I thank God for the wonderful charisms and gifts of *all* the holy religious orders and the legions of saints they've produced. Who cannot be inspired by the glorious lives and loving deeds of St. Benedict and his Benedictines, St. Francis and his Franciscans, St. Ignatius and his Jesuits, and so many more holy orders formed in so many nations across the centuries?

Of course, great saints are not only members of religious orders. In fact, there are great saints from every age since Christ established the Church, from virtually every nation, from both sexes, and from almost every occupation and state in life. Further, there are saints who have suffered and triumphantly endured almost every kind of difficulty, distress, disease, or disorder that you and I might face. There are very good reasons we can track down a patron saint for almost everything! It is most important, per Thomas, that we do track them down, and find what lessons and inspirations they hold for us. We can learn so much from saints with whom we can closely identify and oftentimes who seem so different from us, at least on the surface.

If I might offer a personal example, I am often absorbed in the study of the writings of Sts. Albert the Great and Thomas Aquinas (of course), two of the most profound minds in history. A few years ago, I was asked to deliver a talk on St. Martin de Porres (1579–1639) to a Dominican group. I knew this saint lived in Peru, and I knew that whereas Albert and Thomas are often depicted holding a globe, or a church, or a massive book in their hands, St. Martin is often shown holding a *broom*. I wasn't sure what to expect when I delved into the life of this saint, but what I discovered exceeded my wildest dreams. This great saint of mixed race was a champion of drawing together the rich and the poor and those in between, African slaves, Spanish rulers, and indigenous peoples of Peru. His love of animals would bring a smile to the heart of any Franciscan or Irish saint, and while he was happy to sweep floors, he was also so adept with the surgeon's scalpel that archbishops called upon him when ill. Perhaps my greatest surprise about Martin was that this humble, loving man was also fond of St. Thomas and well-versed in the lessons of the *Summa Theologica*, sometimes providing citations or explanations to seminary students when he overhead them discussing their confusion as he cleaned or swept the floors!

Another saint dear to my heart, and similar to Martin in some ways, is the humble, loving Little Flower, St. Thérèse of Lisieux (1873–1897). How remarkable that this nun who died so young would be named, like Sts. Albert and Thomas, among the few dozen Doctors, or great teachers, of the Church. So would St. Catherine of Siena (1347–1380), though she received no formal education and did not even learn to read until she was in her twenties! (She reported that her reading capacity came as a mystical gift from God, in which Christ appeared to her, accompanied by St. John the Baptist—and our own St. Thomas Aquinas!)

Our space is limited here, and if you will forgive me the thought, I hope, in a sense, that you are disappointed that I did not mention a favorite saint or two of yours. How are we going to follow St. Thomas's advice if we have not immersed ourselves in the lives of our favorite saints? So, I'm really saying that I hope you do have some favorite saints, while remaining always on the lookout for new, unfamiliar saints to inform and inspire you, perhaps toward a life of study, and surely toward a life of holiness.

The saints were indeed a great help to St. Thomas, at times in the most striking ways. Thomas's friend and secretary, Brother Reginald, reported that once Thomas himself became puzzled for days over the interpretation of a text in Isaiah while writing a commentary on that book. One night while he stayed up in his room to pray, Reginald heard Thomas speaking out loud, it seemed to him, with others in his room, though he could not make out the voices or the words they said. Soon after the voices stopped, Thomas called out:

> "Reginald, my son, get up and bring me a light and the commentary on Isaiah; I want you to write for me." So Reginald rose and began to take down the dictation, which ran so clearly that it was as if the master was reading aloud from a book under his eyes.[68]

When Reginald repeatedly asked Thomas about the voices he heard,

Thomas finally replied that Sts. Peter and Paul were sent to him, "and told me all I desired to know."[69]

Of course, the main reason we should imitate the saints is that they all became saintly by imitating Christ. It is Christ, first and foremost, whom they help us imitate, by showing how a life centered on Christ is possible anywhere in the world at any time in history. It was St. Peter who responded when Christ asked him if he would leave Him: "Lord, to whom shall we go? You have the words of eternal life" (John 6:68). It was St. Paul who

---

[68] Antoine Dondaine, *Les Secretaires De Saint Thomas*, 2 vols. (Rome: Editori di S. Tommaso, 1956). As cited in Carruthers, *The Book of Memory*, 5.

[69] Ibid.

declared, "I have been crucified with Christ; it is no longer I who live, but Christ who lives in me" (Gal. 2:20). It is Christ, you will recall, whom St. Thomas called the greatest of all teachers, who taught through His words and His deeds. We are all called to imitate Him foremost.

### Do Not Overlook the "Merely" Noble! (Turning Water into Wine)

In his masterwork, the *Summa Theologica*, Thomas respectfully considered the pronouncements of many great saints of the West and the East, from Augustine to Jerome to Pope Gregory the Great to John Chrysostom, Athanasius, Gregory Nazianzen, and so many others. Further, he sought out the truths and the pearls of wisdom in the writings of those who he knew did not possess the fullness of truth of the Catholic Church. These include thinkers such as the Greek pagan Aristotle and the Roman pagans Cicero and Seneca, and many others; the Jewish Maimonides; and the Arab Muslims Averroes and Avicenna. Thomas cherished truths wherever they might be found, and indeed, this is a hallmark of the Catholic Church. Revelation fears no truths of reason, for there is only one truth. Closer to our time, St. John Paul II stated the gist of Thomas's maxim most elegantly:

> Closer scrutiny shows that even in the philosophical thinking of those who helped drive faith and reason further apart there are found at times precious and seminal insights which, if pursued and developed with a mind and heart rightly tuned, can lead to the discovery of truth's way.[70]

[70] John Paul II, *Fides et Ratio*, no. 48.

Some theologians in St. Thomas's day were highly critical of his use of philosophy in general, and Aristotle in particular, for their service to theology.[71] They argued that he was diluting the wine of divine wisdom with the water of human wisdom. Thomas, however, knew that there is only one truth and that the truth of the faith could never be contradicted by reason, but that reason could help draw some people to faith and help clarify theological principles for the faithful. He did not believe that the noble philosophy of noble men diluted the Faith whatsoever, but rather, that "those who use philosophical doctrines in sacred Scripture in such a way as to subject them to the service of faith, do not mix water with wine, but change water into wine."[72]

May we, like St. Thomas, thirst for the clear sparkling waters of reason, and all the more for the wine of sacred wisdom and the wine above all wines that becomes Christ Himself in the Eucharist!

---

## Doctor's Orders

*Prescription for Letting the Saints Go Marching into Your Soul*

### Reflect

Do you have a favorite religious order whose charism calls out to you? If so, have you considered joining as a lay affiliate? Do you have some favorite saints? If so, what have you done lately

---

[71] Perhaps, to some degree, the "fideists" of their day. See the entry on *fideism* in chapter 12.

[72] See section 2.3, ad. 5 in St. Thomas Aquinas, *Commentary on Boethius' On the Trinity*, St. Isidore Forum, https://isidore.co/aquinas/english/BoethiusDeTr.htm#L22.

to imitate them, especially in regard to their pursuit of truth? If not, might you consider seeking out some new saints to learn from and pray to for their intercession? Our world is desperately in need of saintly heroes.

### Read

Have you made time lately to read the life of a saint unfamiliar to you or a new book about an old favorite? There are a slew of biographies to choose from. If you have a penchant for novels, I've found the works of Louis de Wohl as enlightening and inspiring as they are entertaining. (My favorite? Well, as you might guess, *The Quiet Light*, about St. Thomas Aquinas, is surely a top contender.) Have you read lately the writings of the saints themselves—St. Thomas, or a whole world of others? Have you recently read the Gospels or a good book about Jesus Christ? If you would care to imitate Christ, one of the world's greatest spiritual classics is Thomas à Kempis's *Imitation of Christ*. It has come out in countless editions across the centuries, and just recently in a version that also fleshes it out and brings it even more alive with well-researched and well-written fictionalized episodes about the life of Thomas à Kempis and the circumstances surrounding the crafting of this simple, yet profound devotional book. This new work is Timothy E. Moore's *The Imitation of Christ, Book I: With Comments, Edits, and a Fictional Narrative*.

### Remember

How are you doing remembering key ideas from all the precepts we've covered so far? So far, so good? Then, good! So far, not so hot? Worry not! For in our next chapter, the Angelic Doctor will give us his advice on how to perfect our memories and show us just how to do it.

*Chapter 7*

# Loving Truth Regardless of Its Source (and On the Perfection of Memory)

*Do not place value on who says what, but rather, commit to your memory what true things are said.*

## Who Said What?

Thomas's very next maxim is a wonderful complement to and completion of the one of our last chapter. Although we will strive to honor and imitate noble and saintly people, we should also remain aware of every human person's potential fallibility.[73]

---

[73] Exceptions being the pope and Magisterium under certain circumstances. The pope is gifted by the Holy Spirit with infallibility, but only when he speaks *ex cathedra* (from the chair) of Peter as pope, "when, as supreme pastor and teacher of all the faithful—who confirms his brethren in the faith—he proclaims by a definitive act a doctrine pertaining to faith or morals.... The infallibility promised to the Church is also present in the body of bishops when, together with Peter's successor, they exercise the supreme Magisterium, above all in Ecumenical Council." *Catechism of the Catholic Church* (CCC), no. 891. As Thomas himself wrote regarding the pope, he has "authority which is empowered to decide matters of faith finally, so that they may be held by all with unshakeable faith. Now this belongs to the authority of

Further, we will not automatically discount or ignore the sayings or writings of less-than-saintly or ignoble people either! These two ideas capture the essence of Thomas's approach to truth in the *Summa Theologica*. When he draws from the bevy of the great Western and Eastern, Latin and Greek Fathers before him, he considers their pronouncements with the utmost respect, but he also reflects on whether they have provided complete truths regarding the matters at hand. He does not accept them all blindly but peers at their thoughts with laser-like focus and penetration.

The bottom line here is *the truth*, and not merely the authority, holiness, or nobility of the person who speaks it. This leaves us free respectfully to *question* the conclusions of fallible authorities and to *embrace* truth wherever it may be found. I must note one thing about Thomas himself, though. While he indeed valued truth above all else, perhaps due to both his profound sense of gratitude and his astounding powers of memory, when sharing his countless words of wisdom with us, he usually provides both the truths *and* the names of the people he gleaned them from!

This leads us to the second half of Thomas's maxim. When we latch on to an important truth, regardless of its source, we should commit it to memory. Thankfully, Thomas has shown us just how to do this, so now let us let him show us how!

---

the Sovereign Pontiff, to whom the more difficult questions that arise in the Church are referred." *Summa Theologica*, II-II, Q. 1, art. 10. Further, "The universal Church cannot err, since she is governed by the Holy Ghost, who is the Spirit of Truth." Ibid., II-II, Q. 1, art. 90.

## How to Commit Truths to Your Memory

In addition to his intellectual credentials as a profound philosopher and theologian, St. Thomas is perhaps less widely known as one of the world's great masters of memory. He understood how human memory works and wrote about and practiced how to perfect memory by bringing higher powers of thinking into play.

In an opening passage of her fascinating work *The Book of Memory,* modern English professor Mary Carruthers compares descriptions of Albert Einstein and St. Thomas Aquinas, written by men who knew them well. Although there were interesting similarities, one relevant difference stands out. Whereas Einstein, in the twentieth century, was praised most highly for his *creativity,* which led to his great accomplishments in physics, St. Thomas, in the thirteenth century, was praised most highly for his *memory.* It was said that what he once read and grasped, he never forgot.

One reason Thomas's role as a memory master is not widely known is that he writes about it in just *one page* of his over *three-thousand-page Summa Theologica* and almost smack-dab in the middle, in the Second Part of the Second Part, question 49, article 1. There Thomas answers the question of "Whether Memory Is a Part of Prudence." To cut to the chase, he answers a resounding yes!

Now, prudence is an applied intellectual virtue that governs our moral actions. Thomas calls prudence "right reason applied to action," and its job is to find and execute virtuous means of attaining virtuous goals. To think like Aquinas is to think prudently about things that matter, and to do so requires that we not only *use* but also strive to *perfect* our powers of memory.

Thomas's great mentor, St. Albert the Great, also saw memory as an essential part of prudence — in fact, its most essential part, for to achieve moral goals in the future, we must act in the present, guided by what we have learned in the past. As Albert wrote: "Whence we say that among all those things that point toward ethical wisdom, the most necessary is a trained memory, because from past events we are guided in the present and future, and not from the converse."[74]

Note well that St. Albert points to the necessity not merely of memory, but of a "trained" memory. His greatest student, Thomas Aquinas, tersely told us just how to train our memories in four steps, which I've summarized as follows.[75]

1. First, when we wish to remember a thing, we should take some suitable yet unwonted *illustration* of it, since the unwonted strikes us more, and so makes a greater and stronger impression on the mind.

2. Second, whatever we wish to retain in our memory we must carefully put in *order*, so that we may pass easily from one memory to another.

3. Third, we must be *anxious and earnest* about the things we wish to remember, because the more a thing is impressed on the mind, the less it is liable to slip out of it.

4. Fourth, we should *often reflect* on the things we wish to remember. Therefore, when we reflect on a thing frequently, we quickly call it to mind, through passing from one thing to another by a kind of natural order.

So, in a nutshell that will soon mature into the full-grown oak of artificial memory, Thomas recommends that we form mental

---

[74] From *De Bono (On the Good)*, cited in Carruthers, *The Book of Memory*, 275.

[75] *Summa Theologica*, II-II, Q. 49, art. 1, numbers and emphasis added.

*images*, place them in a certain *order*, *concentrate* on them intently, and *rehearse* or *repeat* them often. Seven hundred years and at least as many scientific studies later, any honest modern memory training expert will have to admit that St. Thomas Aquinas got it right!

Now, if we are to *think* more like Aquinas, we'll need to *memorize* things like him, too. So let's flesh out his four points with a memory exercise using his study precepts as our subject matter. Before we begin, invoking the first and third points, I invite you to fire up your powers of *imagination* and of *concentration*. If you follow closely along, I'll guide you right through the second and fourth points too, as we go through things in *order* and *repeat* them a time or two, doing all that is required to perfect our powers of memory just as St. Thomas advises!

## *Welcome to the House of Memory!*

Imagine that you have been invited for the first time to the home of a modern follower of St. Thomas.[76] It's a sprawling ranch house in American's Midwest, within an older neighborhood surrounded by mature maples and oaks. When you reach the *front door*, you see a most unusual sight, as you are greeted by a former American president. It's Theodore Roosevelt. Can you imagine him with that big mustache and spectacles on a chain? Oddly though, he doesn't speak at first, and when he does it is in slow motion. You are certain it is him though, because he's wielding a big stick (like the one from his famous aphorism). You notice it is decorated at the thick end with a painted blood-red heart, and next to it, a painted image of a human brain, with a whole lot of gray matter!

---

[76] OK, I'll admit it's my own — with just a few alterations.

After our good former president lets you in, you step in onto an *entrance mat*. The mat depicts two large hands folded in prayer. Now there's nothing particularly unusual about that, except that the hands are emitting electric sparks that are making your toes tingle through your shoes!

Then you notice a *clear glass panel* next to the front door, and you see something you can't believe that you missed on your way to the front door. There in the front yard sits a medieval religious person's cell where a large man is deep in study, hunched over a great big book. (Could that be St. Thomas himself?) You suspect as well that he must be fond of wine, since the room is full of old bottles of fine vintage wine, in addition to many books.

Facing back into the house you are surprised to find a *portrait on the wall* on the other side of the front door with two related, but very different scenes. In the first scene, on the left side of the painting, two friends smile at each other as one points out to the other a passage in a large book. In the second scene, on the right, the friends are red-faced in the midst of a heated argument, and the book has fallen on the floor.

On the *adjacent wall of the foyer* is a *gun rack*, perhaps an odd place for one, but odder still, you become fascinated by an ancient globe sitting on its top. You can't resist touching the globe, but when you do your fingers penetrate into it and you really have to struggle to pull them back out.

In *the middle of the foyer* you behold a far more pleasant sight, in fact, perhaps the most pleasant sight any of us can ever hope to see. You wonder if this could be a glimpse of the beatific vision, for there stands Jesus Christ Himself beaming at you, surrounded by a smiling group of your very favorite saints.

Overhead you notice a *chandelier*, and upon it you behold a statue of an ancient Greek goddess. Furthermore, she's surrounded by nine very beautiful daughters. You deduce that this must be Mnemosyne (because her name is carved upon the base of the statue), and she is, in fact, the goddess of memory. Those daughters are the "muses," the goddesses of the nine liberal arts. After all, even the ancient Greeks knew darn well that you can't perfect any art at all unless you can remember the skills that you have learned! Oh, and you notice that for some reason, Mnemosyne is holding in her hand and admiring a very large tooth.

You are well aware by now that this Thomist has a most unusual home, and when you glance over to a *mirror on the wall across from the gun rack*, you are most disconcerted when you see not your own reflection, but a big book with legs standing under a powerful electric generator. Under the mirror is a *cushioned bench* and resting upon it sits another piece of furniture, a cupboard to be exact. You're concerned that it might slide off to the floor since it is full to nearly bursting and it stands on a narrow base with no ledge.

The last stop in our Thomist's foyer is *a little drawer under the cushion of the bench* and when you open the drawer you are most surprised to see a frustrated mentalist you know, attempting to show off his powers, but failing. Don't know any mentalists? Don't worry, you need only *imagine* you do. Don't even know what a mentalist is? Don't worry, we are using it according to this dictionary definition: "a magician who performs feats that apparently demonstrate extraordinary mental powers, such as mind-reading." (Of course, in our case, his demonstration does not go so well.)

Well, there you have it! But just what do you have? Let's review this strange scene again as you try to vividly imagine every piece of it within the "mind's eye" or your imagination. Here are the locations: (1) the front door, (2) the doormat, (3) the glass panel next to the door, (4) the portrait on the wall, (5) the gun rack, (6) the center of the foyer, (7) the chandelier overhead, (8) the mirror on the opposite wall, (9) the bench under the mirror, and (10) the drawers in the bench.

Next, let's look at the strange visual images associated with those locations. At the front door you met a *slow-speaking President Theodore Roosevelt* carrying his *big stick* with a *heart* and a *brain* painted on it. The doormat was decorated with *praying hands* emitting *electrical sparks*. Through the glass panel by the front door you saw that medieval religious person's *cell*, and in it St. Thomas himself, a big book, and plenty of bottles of vintage *wine!* Upon the portrait on the wall were two scenes, one of *two friends enjoying a book* and another of the same *two friends arguing.* Sitting upon the gun rack was the *globe* that *entangled* your fingers. In the center of the foyer was *Christ* surrounded by *saints.* Up in the chandelier holding and admiring a *tooth* was the statue of *Mnemosyne.* In the mirror on the other wall you saw that *book standing under* a *power* generator. Upon the cushion bench was that overloaded *cupboard* teetering upon a *base* with *no ledge.* Finally, in a drawer of the same cushioned bench was the *mentalist* whose trick *failed.* Let's lay this out for ease of review.

| Location | Image |
| --- | --- |
| 1. Front door | *Roosevelt speaks slowly and carries stick* |
| 2. Doormat | *Hands in prayer with sparks* |
| 3. Glass panel | *Monk's cell/wine cellar* |
| 4. Portrait | Friends *smiling/arguing* |

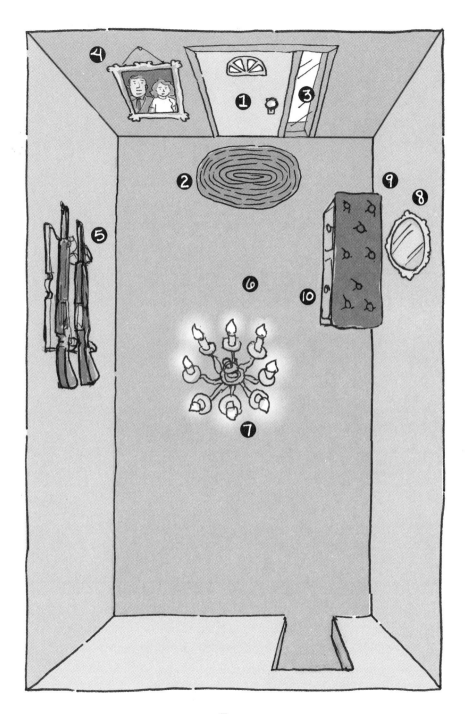

Foyer

| Location | Image |
|---|---|
| 5. Gun rack | *Globe entangles your fingers* |
| 6. Center of foyer | *Christ surrounded by saints* |
| 7. Chandelier | *Tooth admired by Mnemosyne* |
| 8. Mirror | *Book with legs stands under generator* |
| 9. Cushioned bench | *Cupboard on base with no ledge* |
| 10. Drawer | *Mentalist fails at trick* |

So far, so good? If you now know these ten locations and associated images, that's great! If not, do a few more "mental walks" around the foyer until you have them, until you can picture them vividly in your "mind's eye." Got them? Good. If you do, you're very close to knowing and retaining the gist of the ten key precepts from Thomas's "Letter to Brother John" that are found in this book's ten chapters.

This is what we've done. Each of those strange visual images was used to represent and remind us of one of the titles of our chapters which capture the gist of each of Thomas's precepts. Theodore Roosevelt at the front door *speaks slowly* and carries a big stick with a *heart* and *mind* painted on it to remind us of chapter 1's title: "Speak Slowly and Carry a Big Heart and Mind." Roosevelt was used as a reminder of Thomas's advice "to be slow to speak" because the beginning of the president's most memorable phrase — the words "speak softly" — will trigger our altered phrase to "speak *slowly*." We added the images and phrase of a big stick with a heart and a brain painted on it to incorporate the end of his memorable phrase, "and carry a big stick," adding the heart and the brain to remind us of our title's conclusion "and carry a big heart and mind." After all, we aren't training ourselves to be slow to speak in readiness to thump anybody, but rather training our hearts and minds to focus on attaining truth.

The hands in *prayer* emitting *sparks* on the doormat remind us of the second chapter's title "The Power of Pure Prayer." (The sparks are there to remind us of "power.") Thomas *studying* in the *cell* and the *wine cellar* we see through the glass panel in the front yard are reminders of chapter 3's title "From Cell to Wine Cellar: On Crafting a Study Space You Can Love." Our fourth image, the painting with *friends smiling while examining a book* in one panel and *arguing* in the next, will remind us of chapter 4's title: "The Benefits and Perils of Friendliness to Study." That *globe* atop the gun rack of our fifth location *entangled* your fingers as a visual reminder of our chapter 5: "Set Your Intellect Free by Avoiding Worldly Entanglements." (I considered having your brain get entangled in the globe as a more direct reminder for the intellect, but fingers seemed to make a more natural image. Anyway, I hope our image, like your fingers, will stick.)

*Christ* and your favorite *saints* in the center of the foyer (location 6) is a very direct reminder of chapter 6's title: "The Imitation of Christ (and of Those Who Imitate Him)." As for the *tooth* held and admired by *Mnemosyne* up in the chandelier, we use the word "tooth" as a concrete reminder of the abstract word "truth," and the goddess of memory as a reminder of, well, memory. Chapter 7's title is "Loving Truth Regardless of Its Source (and On the Perfection of Memory)." In the mirror (location 8)

# How to Think Like Aquinas

## A Mnemonic Master Table for Thomas's Top-Ten Study Tips

| Location | Image | Chapter Title | Precept Themes |
|---|---|---|---|
| 1. Front Door | Roosevelt speaks slowly; stick | Speak Slowly and Carry a Big Heart and Mind | Listen and think before you speak. |
| 2. Doormat | Prayerful hands emit sparks | The Power of Pure Prayer | Live a life of virtue and prayer. |
| 3. Glass panel | Thomas studies in cell; wine bottles | From Cell to Wine Cellar: On Crafting a Study Space You Can Love | Learn to love the joys of studying. |
| 4. Portrait | Friends smile over book, then argue | The Benefits and Perils of Friendliness to Study | Be friendly, but not too friendly. |
| 5. Gun rack | Globe entangles fingers | Set Your Intellect Free by Avoiding Worldly Entanglements | Don't let worldly things keep you from higher thoughts. |
| 6. Center of foyer | Christ and saints | The Imitation of Christ (and of Those Who Imitate Him) | Imitate Christ, the saints, and the sages. |

| Location | Image | Chapter Title | Precept Themes |
|----------|-------|---------------|----------------|
| 7. Chandelier | Tooth held and admired by Mnemosyne | Loving Truth Regardless of Its Source (and on the Perfection of Memory) | Embrace and memorize important truths. |
| 8. Mirror | Book with legs stands under a power generator | How to Read Any Book: On the Power of Understanding | Fully employ your powers of understanding. |
| 9. Bench | Cupboard rests on base with no ledge | Filling Your Mental Cupboard to the Brim: On Building a Knowledge Base | Never cease seeking to build your knowledge base. |
| 10. Drawers | Mentalist fails at trick | Knowing Your Mental Powers — and their Limits | Exert your intellect to the max, but know that your powers are not limitless. |

you saw that *book* with legs *standing under* a *power* generator to help you remember, in advance, chapter 8's title: "How to Read Any Book: On the Power of Understanding." The book image is pretty straightforward. It is "standing under" to remind us of understanding. The power generator is there of course to visually represent the word "power."

That full *cupboard* on the cushioned bench (location 9) should remind us of the first half of chapter 9's title: "Filling Your Mental Cupboard to the Brim: On Building a Knowledge Base." The *base* with *no ledge* serves as our reminder, of course, for the second half about a knowledge base. Finally, the *mentalist* in the drawer of the bench *fails* at his trick to remind us in advance of chapter 10's title: "Knowing Your Mental Powers—and their Limits."

Do you have all that? If not, just repeat the exercise a time or two, or study just a bit the summary table, remembering all the while that what matters is not exact wording of the chapter titles or precepts, but their underlying meanings, which you might choose to summarize in words of your own.

Now, this method is a form of an ancient memory system called the method of loci (locations) that St. Thomas himself endorsed.[77] The *locations* I present in the table are like a mental

---

[77] Indeed, readers familiar with my book *Memorize the Faith!* (Sophia Institute Press, 2006) will unfailingly recall that when I first introduced this memory foyer, it housed the Ten Commandments. That is why the fifth location of the foyer housed that odd image of a gun rack, which I do not have in my actual foyer. The reason a padlocked gun rack first appeared as our fifth location was to help us memorize the Fifth Commandment. (Yes, you guessed it: "Thou shall not kill!").

And as for the different subject matters, the subtitle of *Memorize the Faith!* began with the words "And Most Anything Else" because these memory methods can be used for memorizing just

notepad that can be used again and again to memorize different subjects. The *images* placed at each location are like the ink in which you can "write" whatever you like upon this notepad in your memory, be they study tips, facts of the Faith, or even the principles of macroeconomics! In fact, in part 2 of this book, you will be shown how to continue to build imaginary memory rooms and to stock them with all kinds of information relevant to thinking like Aquinas, so you'll have them right at hand whenever you need them.

---

## Doctor's Orders ✍

*Prescription for Committing Truths to Memory
Like the Medieval Memory Masters*

### Reflect
Have you come to share St. Thomas's (and St. John Paul II's) respect for truth, whatever its source? Have you learned anything

---

about anything else. I later applied them to books about Catholic apologetics and the rites of the Mass. Further, to my great delight, I found, in a journal of economics and finance, of all places, that *Memorize the Faith!* was listed as a reference in a report on an empirical study demonstrating the power of the mnemonic techniques of the method of loci for college students: M. Shaughnessy and Mary L. White, "Making Macro Memorable: The Method of Loci Mnemonic Technique in the Economics Classroom," *Journal of Economics and Finance Education* 11, no. 2 (Winter 2012): 131–141. Among their conclusions: "An advantage of the method of loci technique is its applicability to any discipline, and students who discover the technique in an economics course likely will find it useful in any other course that requires some amount of memorization" (p. 137) — to which I say, "Amen."

new about the value of and the methods for committing important truths to memory?

## Read

St. Thomas addresses memory as a part of prudence in his *Summa Theologica*, II-II, Q. 49, art. 1. Insights on St. Thomas as a memory master, as well as his teacher St. Albert's complete line-by-line analysis of the *Ad Herennium*, the oldest extant book on these memory methods (ca. 80 B.C.), can be found in Mary Carruthers's *Book of Memory*. My own first and most detailed treatment of these and other memory methods, complete with a book-length tutorial on just how to use them, can be found in *Memorize the Faith! (And Most Anything Else) Using the Methods of the Great Catholic Medieval Memory Masters.*

## Remember

How can we forget this chapter's lessons on memory, of all things? Did you successfully memorize the ten themes of this book's ten chapters? If not, don't despair, for repetitio est mater memoriae (repetition is the mother of memory). Give it another try or two, and I think you will have them down. Further, we've employed the loci technique for fairly complex phrases. Even ancient memory masters distinguished between "memory for words" (rote, word-by-word repetition of phrases) and "memory for things" (the ability to memorize key concepts or ideas). Indeed, it is "memory for things" for which these methods are best suited (as you will see and experience in the exercises in part 2). That's why I suggested that you feel free to memorize the key lessons from each chapter in your own words if you prefer them to mine.

These methods were invented and used by orators who would memorize the key points (not the exact words) of their literary orations, political speeches, or legal arguments, using visual images in an ordered memory system, perhaps even using various features of the very building or forum they spoke in as their location system. This way, as they spoke, they needed merely to glance around them to be reminded of all the important points they wanted to make in their exact order. (That's what I do in all my talks.)

I'll close with a story from a greatly gifted modern orator, a man whose lecture-based program (blackboard, chalk, and all) once led in national television ratings—and, indeed, a man who wrote his doctoral dissertation on the writings of St. Thomas Aquinas!

Venerable Archbishop Fulton J. Sheen (1895–1979) told a story to illustrate why he trained his memory and spoke without notes. While delivering a homily one Sunday, Sheen tells us, a certain bishop paused for quite some time while he noisily shuffled his notes, trying to find his place. To the bishop's chagrin, an elderly parishioner in the pews could contain herself no longer and called out for all to hear, "How does he expect us to remember all of this when he can't remember it himself?"

*Chapter 8*

# How to Read Any Book: On the Power of Understanding

*Try to understand whatever you read and*
*to verify whatever is doubtful.*

## *Thomas and Thomists Proclaim the Power of Reading*

The prolific twentieth-century philosopher Mortimer J. Adler once wrote a book entitled *How to Read a Book*. Many jokingly asked him how anybody could read *his* book if they did not *already know* how to read a book. Adler would then point out the subtitle: "The Art of Getting a Liberal Education." His book, of course, was not a primer on how to read, but a guide to reading more effectively and to reading the kinds of books that liberate and educate the mind. He also had the last laugh, so to speak, since that book became his best seller!

His book was, in a sense, a lengthy explication of the first part of this precept from Thomas's letter on study. Indeed, Adler was a great admirer of St. Thomas Aquinas and considered himself a Thomist. Further, although he was born into a Jewish family and called himself a "pagan" throughout most of his adult life, Adler became a Christian in his seventies, and he died in his nineties as a member of the Catholic Church. Talk about a man devoted to study and following the truth wherever it might lead him! Indeed, in my forties, Adler's books *How to Think about God* and *The Difference of Man and the Difference It Makes* led me to read St. Thomas for the first time, which, in turn, brought me back to God and the Catholic Church!

The right kind of reading opens us to deep reservoirs of knowledge. Following St. Thomas's earlier advice, we can start with narrow streams of slim and accessible books as we work our way over time to drink of the deepest knowledge that larger, loftier tomes, such as the works of St. Thomas, contain!

## Understanding Makes All the Difference

Thomas knew well that the power to understand defines us as human beings. He would write in his masterwork that "the nature of each thing is shown by its operation. Now the proper operation of man as man is to understand; because he thereby surpasses all other animals."[78] This power of understanding is the fundamental "difference of man" that Adler, too, believed makes all the difference. It is the fundamental fact of our human nature. Further, as modern-day Thomist Dr. Peter Redpath points out: "Since human nature is the proximate principle of all the reasoning principles that flow from it, being wrong about human nature will never generate a correct understanding of philosophy, science, metaphysics, ethics, or religion (including Catholicism.)"[79]

---

[78] *Summa Theologica*, I, Q. 72, art. 1.

[79] Peter Redpath, *The Moral Psychology of St. Thomas Aquinas: An Introduction to Ragamuffin Ethics* (St. Louis: En Route Books, 2017), 32.

Dr. Redpath was not the first to make such a claim, though (nor was St. Thomas). Aristotle hinted at it more than 2,300 years ago when he noted that "acquaintance with the soul would seem to help much in acquiring all truth, especially about the natural world; for it is, as it were, the principle of living things."[80] St. Thomas was well aware of Aristotle's opinion, too, since he wrote a detailed commentary on every line of Aristotle's book *De Anima* (*On the Soul*), from which that statement comes. Thomas himself argued that we cannot know proper moral behaviors, for example, unless we understand the powers of the soul; we cannot reason about the highest, most divine immaterial things unless we understand the immaterial powers of our intellects; and we cannot properly understand living things unless we understand how all their actions originate in the soul.

If we want to think like Aquinas, we must pay serious attention to what he thought about the nature of understanding. Indeed, the operation of understanding is what distinguishes us from every other animal on earth and is one important way in which we were made in the image and likeness of God. So let's take a whirlwind tour of Thomas's understanding of understanding. It will help us understand whatever we read—and everything else in ourselves and the world as well!

## The Nature of Human Nature

Perhaps you have heard of the "mind-body problem" in philosophy and psychology. How can the purely mental events of our minds impact the separate physical realities of our bodies, and vice versa? The British atheistic philosopher Bertrand Russell

---

[80] St. Thomas Aquinas, *Commentary on Aristotle's* De Anima (Notre Dame, IN: Dumb Ox Books, 1994), 1.

once dismissed the issue with a quip: "What is mind? It doesn't matter. What is matter? Never mind!" Great thinkers throughout the ages have held a variety of views on this key issue of human nature, some of which pitted the mind against the body or collapsed them into one. Plato, for example, believed that we are essentially spiritual souls trapped within material bodies while on earth. Others, such as Democritus in ancient times and many people today who consider themselves scientific, believe we are nothing but matter, and that the mind, let alone the soul, is an old-fashioned fiction. Aquinas could not disagree more with both of those views. He says that the body and *soul* (a broader term than *mind*, but one that encompasses it), are not two separate natures within us but together form the composite unity that is a human being. Aristotle had tersely noted fifteen hundred years before Thomas, "We can dismiss the question of whether the soul and body are one; it is as though we were to ask whether the wax and its shape are one."[81]

Thomas gives the question a thorough answer. He notes, "Matter is that which is not as such 'a particular thing,' but is in mere potency to become a 'particular thing.' Form is that by which a 'particular thing' actually exists. And the compound is the 'particular thing' itself."[82] The soul is the form of the body — that gift from God which makes us particular human beings.[83]

---

[81] On the Soul, bk. 2, chap. 12; cited in *The Complete Works of Aristotle: The Revised Oxford Translation*, ed. Jonathan Barnes (Princeton, NJ: Princeton University Press, 1984), 657.

[82] Aquinas's *Commentary on* De Anima (On the Soul), bk. 2, chap. 1, cited in *Aquinas on Human Nature*, ed. Thomas S. Hibbs (Indianapolis, IN: Hackett, 1999), 19.

[83] This is the official teaching of the Church as well. See CCC 365.

A word about perfection, which St. Thomas uses in a specific way: to be perfect is, literally, to be complete. In Latin, *per* plus *factus* means "thoroughly made." God is perfect in that He is complete in every attribute, fully actualized, pure spirit without matter, and therefore, immutable or unchangeable. Thomas says that in matter, there are four degrees of perfection: (1) existence, (2) living, (3) sensing, and (4) understanding. As living human beings, you and I reach all four. Your concrete driveway has attained only the first degree, which in itself is good—for Thomas echoes God in the book of Genesis that "all that exists is good." And yet your driveway can't do much more than lie there for cars to park on, because it does not have a soul. But do those irksome weeds by it have a soul? St. Thomas answers with an unequivocal yes, though in a specific and relatively limited sense. Of course, our interest here is in the nature of man and the human soul, and not that of the cement or the weeds in our driveway, but they do provide us with our starting point on the road to understanding the human soul—including its unique powers of understanding!

We sometimes call nonliving things at the first level of perfection *inanimate* objects, and living things at the next three levels *animate* objects. That is thinking like Aquinas, because *anima* is Latin for "soul." The weeds by your driveway, like the daffodils and trees nearby, are indeed alive and therefore have a soul—a *vegetative soul*, fitting for vegetables and for all forms of plant life! The rock or asphalt in your driveway has no soul, but the weeds and any kind of plant life do, since that is the most basic function of soul, to be the "form" that gives life to the matter of a living being's physical body. This life-giving vegetative soul has three main powers: (1) nutrition, (2) growth, and (3) reproduction. (You might notice at this point that *you* also possess these three powers.)

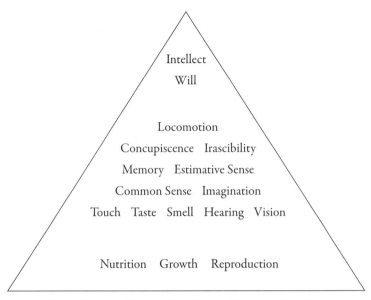

**Vegetative, Sensitive, and Intellectual Powers of the Soul**

Now, to get out of the weeds and down to the business of our human powers, I direct your attention to the diagram "Vegetative, Sensitive, and Intellectual Powers of the Soul." We have started with the three powers of the vegetative soul, powers that form the apex of the pyramid of the soul of plant life, but merely the lowest foundation of the human soul. Every mature living plant, animal, or human on earth without some unusual deficiency or defect has, by its nature, those powers to nourish itself, to grow and repair tissue, and to reproduce its own kind. Indeed, while moderns might ponder how a spiritual soul (or at least a "mind") can arise from a material body, in a very real sense, *one of the soul's most fundamental acts is to grow the appropriate body!*

Moving a crucial rung up this pyramid of perfection, we come to the level of the sensitive soul, which critters such as your dog or cat possess. As fond as they may be of eating, growing, or finding mates, chances are they do many other things besides. After all, that's why you chose them, and not tomato plants, to be your family pets. And of course, the distinguishing characteristic of a *sensitive soul* does not merely mean that it can get grumpy or be easily slighted. It refers to the fact that animals—but not plants—possess the powers of sensation.

The first of these is touch, and some primitive animals may possess it without the other four senses. One of Thomas's examples is that of the homely oyster. Our human powers of touch are very well developed, and we can use them to sense all kinds of things, such as heat, pressure, vibration, and more. Of course, our dogs and cats share the powers of touch with us as they do the other four senses of smell, taste, hearing, and vision. In fact, my dogs can smell and hear a lot better than I can, and I'd wager that the same applies to yours. Also, we and other animals have very obvious bodily organs that serve these five senses—skin, noses, tongues, ears, and eyes—along with the less obvious nerve networks and brain centers to which they connect.

## Beyond the "Sixth Sense" to the Seventh, Eighth, and Ninth

Our five external senses provide the pathways to knowledge and understanding, but they are far from the end of the road in themselves. Please allow me to illustrate with a simple scenario.[84]

---

[84] You may have seen a variant of this scenario in my books *The One-Minute Aquinas: The Doctor's Quick Answers to Fundamental Questions* (Sophia Institute Press, 2014) and *Unearthing Your Ten Talents: A Thomistic Guide to Spiritual Growth through the Virtues and the Gifts* (Sophia Institute Press, 2009). If you already know the answer, please don't spoil it for new readers!

I see two patches of white, hear flapping sounds, feel dampness, smell a musty odor, and taste a hint of salt. Whatever could it be? My senses have not told me much else. Now I perceive that each patch stands about one foot tall, is just a few inches from me, has four downward tubular projections, and one in the back that is moving quickly from side to side. Still don't know what they are? Then let me introduce you to our dogs Lily and Lucy, who have just come inside from playing in wet snow and are shaking themselves dry.

Note how the disparate bits of information coming in from our separate external senses don't necessarily make much sense until they are all put together and integrated by what St. Thomas called the *sensus communis* or "common sense." He is not talking about the kind of practical, down-to-earth, common sense that your parents always encouraged you to use, but a special, synthesizing power of the human and higher animal soul. It is this common sense that enables us to perceive as one thing (two in this example!) the many data provided by our diverse external senses. In modern psychological terminology, the senses produce *sensation*, but the common sense — the first of what Thomas calls the four internal senses, produces *perception*. Perception derives from the Latin word *percipere*, "to seize wholly" (as a whole, unified thing — in this case the two whole things, our dogs Lily and Lucy).

So, the common sense does indeed make sense, but so do three other internal senses in the same tier of our pyramid. I'll bet you've formed some kind of fuzzy mental image of little Lily and Lucy, have you not? To help you a bit, Lily is a five-year-old miniature American Eskimo. She is a fourteen-pound bundle of energy encased in thick, fluffy snow-white fur. Lucy, age nine, also a miniature, with sleek, silvery white hair, is very laid back, a twenty-pound "couch-cuddler" with the classic bearded snout that earned her breed the name of Schnauzer. The mental images[85] you have now formed are courtesy of a second internal sense called, quite appropriately, *imagination*. Indeed, Aristotle believed that "the soul never thinks without an image,"[86] and the Angelic Doctor agreed.

Humans and higher animals have the power to hold on to sense perceptions after the objects that produced them are no longer present to act on the sense organs. This basic power of forming images, as we just saw, is called *imagination*. We can say that the five external senses and the common sense are "presentational" powers, since they convey and present to us particular things that are present in the world outside us (and at times, too, things present in the world *within* us, as when we hear not our dogs but our stomachs growling). The internal sense of imagination is the first of our "re-presentational" powers, since the images serve as re-presentations of original experiences that free us from the immediate present. We can imagine Lily and Lucy, for example, even when they're not hanging around. Further, the imagination has another very imaginative trick up its sleeve: its ability to combine and form images of things that we have never experienced. Nobody has ever seen an American Eskimo or a Schnauzer as big as a house (thank God!), but we can easily imagine them. We can create novel imaginary images, too, by combining in various ways the images of virtually anything we have ever seen — or imagined!

---

[85] "Phantasms" in Aristotle's Greek, deriving from the word *phos*, meaning "light."

[86] *On the Soul*, bk.3, chap. 7.

A third internal sense is *memory*. Also re-presentational, it builds up powers of the imagination with temporal, emotional, and intellectual components. Through the power of memory, we realize that the objects of our images are not only absent, but they happened in the past. Our personal memories are also embedded in the context of the emotional experiences in which they occurred. Call to mind your grandmother or your best childhood friend, and you are likely to feel something, too.

And for human beings, the intellect also comes into play. Surely you will recall from our last chapter that not only can we hold on to past impressions via sensory memory, as do other animals, but we possess powers of recollection, whereby the thinking powers of the highest tier of our pyramid reach down, so to speak, and give us a hand in figuring out strategies for recalling old things and remembering new ones. Further, we can remember not only particular things we have sensed in the past but also universal concepts and abstract ideas, as we shall soon consider.

Animals and humans share in a final, most vital inner sense. Not only do we perceive things as having certain sensible qualities; we also perceive whether they are *good* or *bad*, desirable or undesirable, and useful or harmful to us. In animals, this is called the estimative sense (*vis aestimativa*) or animal prudence. St. Thomas notes that the lamb senses not only things such as the size, shape, color, sound, and smell of the wolf; it senses the *dangerousness* of the wolf, which is not present in the information derived from the external senses alone. This estimative sense is the cognitive component of instinct.

Even we humans are naturally attracted to or repelled by some objects before we have time to reflect upon them with our intellects. (In my own case, the sudden presence of a snake would trigger this response; for my wife, a mouse does the trick.)[87]

In humans, this important power, so crucial to the preservation of life, is also subject to guidance by the intellect. It is called the cogitative sense (*vis cognitiva*) or "particular reason." It is called particular reason because it is subject to guidance by the reasoning powers of the intellect (to be addressed later), but its focus is on particular things, rather than on universal concepts.

As the common sense integrates the information from the five external senses, so too does the cogitative sense integrate the information from the external senses *and* the higher-order internal senses of the common sense, imagination, and memory, leaving the cogitative sense but one step removed from the powers of the intellectual soul.

There you have it: a brief look at the internal senses. But more remains in this tier of our pyramid within the sensitive powers of the soul.

## Hooked on a Feeling? Do the Locomotion

The estimative or cogitative sense that allows Lily and Lucy, or you and me, to determine that certain things are good for us or bad for us sure wouldn't serve much purpose if all we could do is sit there like a rutabaga, calm and content all the time, rooted to one spot in the earth. Two more fundamental powers of the sensitive soul separate the animal and the plant worlds.

---

[87] My wife was just reading over my shoulder while proofing this, and she does not dispute it! (And, strange as it seems to me, she does not hesitate to handle snakes when offered the chance at the zoo, to which offers I say, "No, thank you.")

The first are the source of what Thomas called the "passions" and what we are more likely to call emotions or feelings. Even though we may experience them intensely, and they may motivate us to action, Thomas uses the word "passion" because the word implies passivity, in the sense that our bodies and souls have receptivity—the ability to be influenced by the objects we perceive outside ourselves, whether to draw us toward them (as in the passion of love) or repel us (as in the passion of hate), while members of the plant world just sit there soaking up the sunshine and drawing in nutrients, unmoved by anything else.

Our pets and the beasts in the wild have passions, though, and so do we. The passions are movements of the sensitive appetites of the soul when we are faced with good or evil. The two primary powers that produce all our passions are the *concupiscible* appetite, fueled by love, whereby we have an affinity for the good and are repelled by evil, and the *irascible* appetite, fueled by hate in the sense that it motivates us to remove obstacles barring us from the things we love. In the last analysis, love conquers all and is the primary passion that moves us, since even the passions of the irascible appetite, as noted above, serve to remove whatever obstacles come between us and the things that we love.

We can see these appetites very clearly in action in the animal world, where so much behavior is motivated by the concupiscible appetite toward seeking the goods of food, mates, and territory (which provides access to food and mates), while most aggression is motivated by the irascible appetite, centered on conflicts over those same goods. Humans, too, have such appetites, as I'm sure you will agree from your own experience. Again, as is the case for many higher sensitive powers, though, while animals are guided by instinct and training, our higher reasoning capacities can step in to regulate these appetites (though it is not always easy).

Finally, for the powers of the sensitive soul, it is time to do the locomotion, so to speak. Having appetites and aversions would be of no use if we did not have a means to act on them, to go after good things and flee or fight against evils. Aristotle argued that nature does not act in vain, and St. Thomas agreed. This final power of the sensitive soul is that of locomotion or self-movement. Unlike plants and all but some of the simplest of animals rooted to one spot, animals and humans are able to move about, moving their whole bodies or limbs to seek or avoid things as they see fit.

So much, then, for a brief introduction to the powers of the sensitive soul. It is time to take the most crucial leap up our pyramid of powers of the soul to the peak, from which only humans among all species on earth have the capacity to oversee and to guide the other powers. We'll start at the top.

## *The Intellectual Soul and the Road to Understanding*

The thinking capacities of animals stop at the level of phantasms or images. These images capture and re-present particular things and events or particular dogs, such as Lily, for example. But we can speak of dogs in general, too. You have probably never met Lily, but you understand what I mean when I talk about her. In fact, as for all the words I use in this book, you either understand them, or if you don't, you possess the capacity to ask someone what they mean or to look them up. Dogs, such as Lily and Lucy, and all other animal species (even parrots) produce no words of their own. Further, you and I can also talk about abstractions, such as truth, justice, and the American way, even though we can't see, hear, touch, taste, or smell them. This is the gift of the intellectual soul, and it possesses two main powers that allow us to grasp abstract, universal, and immaterial realities.

Just as the internal senses produce images from sense impressions, the agent or active intellect produces abstractions from those images. The Latin word *intellectus* derives from *intus* (inside) and *legere* (to read). The *agent intellect* looks below the surface of experience to abstract (draw forth) the essences of objects that have stimulated our senses. It sorts the jumble of sensory data to perceive a thing's essential, universal nature. The agent intellect's gaze is unobstructed by particular, accidental features; it's like an X-ray that looks through the externals to see the reality below the appearance. My eyes look at little, fluffy Lily and at sturdy, bearded Lucy, her Schnauzer "sister," and my agent intellect detects the quiddity—the "whatness," or, in this case, the substantial "dog-ness"—that they share, despite their accidental, nonessential differences. The *abstraction* produced by the agent intellect is *form without matter*. It is *immaterial* and not the product of any particular bodily organ (not even the brain), as the products of the senses are, as will be spelled out in our next section.

But the intellect has not finished its workings on their white fluffy or silky furriness.

The last stop on the road to human understanding is the *possible intellect*.[88] Just as the percepts of the senses and common sense provide the data for images, the abstractions of the agent intellect

---

[88] Strictly speaking, Thomas does not say we have two intellects, but two primary *powers* of the intellect used in concept formation. This intellectual power may also be referred to as the *passive* or *potential* intellect. In Thomas's Latin it is *intellectus possibilis*.

provide the fodder for the ideas or concepts of the possible intellect. The abstraction is then received by the powers of the possible intellect, which stimulates it to produce a product of its own, which we call a concept or idea. Get the idea?[89] Maybe this will help:

**The Road to Understanding**

| Level of Soul | Power | Product |
|---|---|---|
| Sensitive | External senses | Sensation |
| | Common sense | Perception |
| | Imagination | Phantasm (or image) |
| | Memory | |
| | Cogitative sense | |
| Intellectual | Agent intellect | Abstraction |
| | Possible intellect | Idea (or concept) |

[89] It is a very crucial one, and we'll encounter some of its misunderstandings in chapter 12. Many modern philosophers and psychologists since the days of John Locke in the seventeenth century have cast doubt on the powers of the mind by supposing that ideas are the objects of our thinking, or *that which we think about*, thus severing the direct connection between our ideas and the outside world. St. Thomas makes clear that things themselves are the objects of our ideas and our ideas are primarily a means, or *that by which we think about things*, although we *also* possess the self-reflective capacity to think about our thinking, when we are so inclined.

Maybe it will help a little more to view this as a process:

### The Birth of an Idea[90]

| | Thing or object | | | |
|---|---|---|---|---|
| Faculties | Outer sense and Common sense ↓ | Imagination Memory Cogitative sense | Agent intellect | Possible intellect |
| *Product* | *Percept →* | *Phantasm →* | *Abstraction →* | *Concept or idea* |
| Description | Impressed sensible species | Expressed sensible species | Impressed intelligible species | Expressed intelligible species |

## *Immaterial Thoughts, Indestructible Soul*

Let's note that as we move along the road to human understanding, we start with *particular things* and end with *universal ideas*. We start with the sensations produced by *material*, bodily organs, and end with concepts of a purely *spiritual*, intellectual soul. In sensations, forms are separated from matter, but not from the conditions of particular material things: if you *see* a rock, you see it because it's sitting in front of you. In the ideas of the intellect, forms are separated from matter and from its particular conditions as well: if you're *thinking* about rock in general, *your mind*

---

[90] Adapted from, Robert E. Brennan, *Thomistic Psychology* (New York: MacMillan, 1941), 183.

"sees" an image of rock, whether one is in front of you or not. Sensations are particular and concrete; ideas are universal and abstract. Since the intellect can potentially know the essence of *all* material bodies, it cannot itself be a material organ.[91] As Thomas points out:

> If the intellectual soul were composed of matter and form, the forms of things would be received into it as individuals, and so it would only know the individual; just as it happens with the sensitive powers which receive forms in a corporal organ; since matter is the principle by which forms are individualized. It follows, therefore, that the intellectual soul—and every intellectual substance which has knowledge of forms absolutely—is exempt from composition of matter and form.[92]

Let's note one other important implication of the immateriality of the human intellectual soul—in fact, it's the most important of all possible implications. Because the human soul is *immaterial*, it has no parts that can decompose. Barring an act of annihilation by God Himself, *the soul is also immortal*. How important it is, then, to act in ways pleasing to God, who breathed immortality into our spiritual souls!

---

[91] Since humans are soul-body composites, the soul is indeed supplied with phantasms by bodily organs, such as the sense organs, which send information to our brains. Thus, damage to those material organs can hinder the spiritual intellect from forming new ideas and performing other intellectual operations, such as judgment and reasoning.

[92] *Summa Theologica*, I, Q. 75, art. 5.

## *Where There's a Free Will, There's a Uniquely Human Way*

Perhaps you've noticed one last power near the top of the pyramid yet to be explained. Very good then; we've got one last bit of explaining to do. We've seen how the intellectual powers of the human soul are unique among those of all creatures on earth. Being composites of material bodies and spiritual souls, we have a uniquely human way of knowing that is inaccessible to irrational animals. Angels have higher intellects. As purely spiritual beings, their knowledge of what things are comes all at once to them as instantaneous intuition. They don't require sensory data and the multiple steps of cognitive processing and reasoning that we do.[93] Human beings not only have a unique way of *knowing*; we have a unique way of *acting* as well. If we want to know which human acts lead to happiness, we must learn about the human *will*. And since there's a will, you can rest assured that St. Thomas has provided a *way* to understand it.

Questions 1–21 in the First Part of the Second Part of the *Summa Theologica* address such issues of human acts, taking more than a hundred pages to do so. Here, we'll give you the highlights.

*Voluntas* — the will — is a uniquely human power. It's such an important subject in understanding our freedom and our salvation that St. Thomas uses the word in ways that are more exacting than our colloquial understanding of will as "whatever I happen to want at the moment." As the intellect seeks to know the *true*, the will seeks to obtain the *good*. The intellect operates

---

[93] Readers intrigued by angels will delight in the Angelic Doctor's treatise about them, including their unique thinking capacities. *Summa Theologica*, Qs. 50–64.

in the realm of *knowledge*, and the will in the realm of *love*. The intellect *discerns* what is good, and the will *acts* to get it. The will is *the capacity to desire what is truly good*. Hold on! In the everyday sense, we know that we *can* desire the truly good — but we don't always pursue it. But first things first: without a will, we couldn't even desire it.

Since the ultimate goal, or *end*, of man is the attainment of happiness, there is a sense in which the will itself is not free, since no one can truly desire unhappiness. Augustine says, "All desire happiness with one will," and Thomas agrees, saying, "The will desires something of necessity."[94] This does not mean, as some modern deterministic psychologists and philosophers hold, that we have no free will, that our acts are determined for us and are not our responsibility. Indeed, Thomas retorts to deniers of free will, "*I answer that*, Man has free will: otherwise counsels, exhortations, commands, prohibitions, rewards, and punishments would be in vain."[95]

If the will is *necessitated* to desire the good, how, then, can we have *free* will? Thomas says that the "proper act" of free will is *choice*. We have *freedom of exercise* to choose whether to employ our wills and make a choice one way or another in a given situation. (Surely procrastinators can relate to this!) We have *freedom of specification* to select one thing or course of action while rejecting others. Our free choice is not in regard to the ultimate

[94] *Summa Theologica*, I, Q. 82, art. 1.

[95] Ibid., I, Q. 83, art. 1. For an interesting look at the claims of some neuroscientists and social psychologists who claim on the basis of very simple and flawed experiments that they have disproved the existence of free will, I recommend Alfred R. Mele, *Free: Why Science Hasn't Disproved Free Will* (New York: Oxford University Press, 2014).

end or goal: we want happiness. What we choose is the *means to that end*. It is through our ability to choose or not to choose between different means that we exercise free will and become active, nondetermined agents—masters of our own actions and worthy of praise or of blame.

## *On Verification*

If Brother John (or you and I) truly want to grow in knowledge, we will strive to arrive at the *meaning* of whatever material we read. To read a book requires so much more than sounding out phonetically the words on the printed page. We must not be like parrots repeating the author's words without knowing what they mean. We need to read carefully to understand what an author means. For unfamiliar words, we may need to consult a dictionary or a learned friend.

Further, once we have grasped[96] the gist of the author's statements, we need to ask ourselves, "Is it true?" There is an old saying that "you can't believe everything you read in the newspapers," and an updated version that "you can't believe everything you read on the Internet."

---

[96] If I might digress a bit, our word "comprehend" derives from the Latin *prehendere*, "to take hold of, or grasp." Indeed, most of our common English words for the abstract thinking operations of the intellect reveal their foundations in the sensations and motions of the physical body and the sensitive powers of the soul, just as Thomas taught. "Consider" is from *sidera*, "to gaze at" the stars; "reflect" is from *reflectere*, "to bend back"; "discern" is from *circus*, to mark off with "a circle or ringed area"; and "cogitate" is from *agitare*, "to shake up or turn over." Fr. Brennan provides these and five more examples in Robert Edward Brennan, *Thomistic Psychology: A Philosophic Analysis of the Nature of Man* (New York: Macmillan, 1941).

As Catholics, we believe in one special infallible book (collection of books, more precisely): the Bible, of course, as understood and interpreted authoritatively by the Church. We do not doubt the Bible's contents, but even so, we are not merely a "people of the book." Christ did not write a book; He founded a Church, which later provided us with the books inspired by God. Further, an old saying goes, "I fear the man of one book," and, interestingly, it is often attributed to none other than St. Thomas Aquinas![97] In other words, we should fear those who are overspecialized, whose views may be excessively narrow, failing to understand any subject completely by being blind to how it relates to the web of other truths that put it into full context. As for our precept here, if we read something doubtful, one method to verify its truth is to consult other reliable sources, perhaps with other conclusions, and then to submit the issue to our own reasoning powers. We can also acquaint ourselves with common logical fallacies and erroneous ideological assumptions that can lead arguments astray.[98] In terms of factual matters, this can sometimes be done by controlled observations or experiments, the stuff of the scientific method. Thomas was well aware of it in his day. His great mentor, after all, St. Albert the Great, is the patron saint of scientists! In

[97] I have not been able to pinpoint this in his writings myself. A quick Internet search yields Thomist Dr. Taylor Marshall's thoughts on the matter (though he could not find it either!). Dr. Taylor Marshall, "Did Thomas Aquinas Fear the Man of One Book?" *Taylor Marshall, Ph.D.* (blog), August 10, 2015, http://taylormarshall.com/2015/08/did-thomas-aquinas-fear-the-man-of-one-book.html.

[98] This is the stuff of chapters 11 and 12.

terms of theological matters, we turn to the teaching Magisterium of the Catholic Church.[99]

---

## Doctor's Orders 🖋

*Prescription for Unlocking Understanding*

### Reflect

We covered a lot of ground in this chapter, and hopefully it has provided us with a firm foundation for a better understanding of ourselves and, therefore, of everything else! Here is a little thinking exercise for you. Thomas, in his writings on the virtue of prudence, spoke of a "twofold" power of understanding, both the power to grasp universal ethical principles (such as "do the good") and the power to understand the nature of particular things or choices we face to determine whether they truly embody "the good" in a particular situation. These can be seen as the universal and singular premises of an ethical syllogism, to put it abstractly, something like this:

I should do the good (universal premise).

This particular course of action is (or is not) good (singular premise).

Therefore, I should (or should not) pursue it (conclusion).

Think of a challenging practical situation you recently faced, something that required you to choose between actions to achieve your goal in your academic, work-related, or personal life. Can you look back on your "twofold" powers of understanding in action

---

[99] The stuff of chapter 13.

by ferreting out the kinds of universal and singular premises you used to arrive at your decision about what to do?[100] You might even consider writing them down. Next, do you face some kind of decision right now, or will you in the near future, that will require a prudent decision on your part? If so, what kind of universal and singular premises apply to that situation, and how might you use your powers of memory and understanding to make the most prudent decision?

**Read**

Thomas's analysis of understanding as a part of prudence is in his *Summa Theologica*.[101] His explanation of the nature of man and the powers of the soul can be found in his *Commentary on Aristotle's* De Anima (On the Soul) and in the *Treatise of Man*.[102] The most clear and helpful book I have found on these issues is in Robert Brennan, O.P., Ph.D.'s *Thomistic Psychology: A Philosophic Analysis of the Nature of Man*. Another good and easy read on the subject is Mortimer J. Adler's *Intellect: Mind Over Matter*.[103] Finally, a more challenging but worthwhile book, hot off the presses in 2017, is Dr. Peter Redpath's aforementioned *Moral Psychology of St. Thomas Aquinas: An Introduction to Ragamuffin Ethics*.

---

[100] Both kinds of premises could vary widely depending on your circumstances. Universal premises, for instance, might involve the value of pursuing higher education while balancing family obligations, and the singular premise might involve particular programs at particular schools.

[101] *Summa Theologica*, II-II, Q. 49, art. 2.

[102] Ibid., I, Qs. 75–89.

[103] Mortimer Jerome Adler, *Intellect: Mind over Matter* (New York: Macmillan, 1990).

**Remember**

Never forgetting that rehearsal is the mother of memory, let's start by reviewing our memory foyer again. Do you recall all ten locations and images and the precepts that they contain? If not, it's time for a little more rehearsal. Another repetition or two should help lock them all in and warm us up for the heavy-duty memory work we'll do in part 2.

# Chapter 9

# Filling Your Mental Cupboard to the Brim: On Building a Knowledge Base

*Put whatever you learn into the cupboard of your
mind as if you were filling a cup to the brim.*

## Fill'er Up, Please — with Knowledge

Again, we see a nod to the power and importance of memory. In his opening statement to Brother John, Thomas recommended acquiring a *thesauro scientiae*, a storehouse or hoard of treasures of knowledge. Here our metaphor moves to the mind as a storehouse of intellectual food and as a cup to be filled with the fine wine of knowledge. What is worth learning is worth remembering, and a trained memory will supply us with a place for everything and will supply everything with a place. Indeed, Thomas was well aware that, centuries before him, St. Jerome, commenting on the passage in which Ezekiel was told by God, "eat this scroll" (Ezek. 3:1), wrote:

> Eating the book is the starting-point of reading and of basic history. When, by diligent meditation, we store away the book of the Lord in our memorial treasury, our belly is filled spiritually and our guts are satisfied.... Nothing

that you have seen or heard is useful, however, unless you deposit what you should see and hear in the treasury of your memory.[104]

Note, too, Thomas's admonition to fill our cups to the brim. We should be so thirsty for truth that no half-filled cup will do! Bl. Humbert of Romans, who served as Dominican master general during Thomas's adulthood, borrowing from St. Bernard of Clairvaux, wrote that preachers should not be like a pipe that receives and pours all at once, but like a bowl that fills up and then overflows, sharing its contents with others. We, too, should emulate the good preacher, by striving always to fill our cups of knowledge. Truly, no one can learn everything, but God has crafted our finite intellects with such vast storage capacities that we can truly strive for the rest of our lives to fill our mental storehouse with truths and never need worry about running out of room. An old Jewish saying holds that even a bushel filled to the brim with nuts can hold further measures of oil.

### The Power of a Broad, Sturdy Knowledge Base

Modern psychologists would call the process of filling mental cupboards to the brim building a broad *knowledge base*. You've heard the old saying that "the rich get richer, and the poor get poorer."[105] There is a sense in which this principle operates in our capacities to learn and think. We learn new things by making connections with things we already know, like the narrow

---

[104] St. Jerome, *Commentary on Ezekiel*, cited in Carruthers, *The Book of Memory*, 44.

[105] "For to everyone who has will more be given, and he will have abundance; but from him who has not, even what he has will be taken away" (Matt. 25:29).

streams that eventually lead to broad seas in Thomas's metaphor. The more things you know, the easier it is to make new connections and to learn even more. The accumulation of what one learns over time is one's knowledge base. Thomas's knowledge base was like a mountain base—and the whole mountain on top of it! Any of us who try, though, can build our own knowledge base, especially if we employ memory and study methods like the ones we encountered in chapter 7.

A broad knowledge base even has practical advantages in helping us "think on our feet" and make hard real-world decisions. Once we have built a firm base of knowledge and experience, we will be better prepared to make quick decisions and act quickly when faced with the unexpected. We will have more resources to draw on. The broader and sturdier we've built our knowledge base, the more likely those swift decisions will be sound ones.

An interesting study on the power of a knowledge base was reported in the 1970s.[106] A group of ten-year-olds was pitted against a group of adults on two kinds of memory tasks, one a test of ability to recall random ten-digit numbers, and the second involving memorization of the positions of chess pieces. When it came to digit recall, adults won, as was expected. (The average recall for adults is about seven digits in order; for ten-year-olds, it is about six.) Still, the children recalled the chess-piece positions better than the adults because they, and not the adults, were regular chess players. In other words, though their raw memory capacities were not yet as strong as those of the adults, the power of the

---

[106] M.T.H. Chi, "Knowledge Structures and Memory Development," in *Children's Thinking: What Develops?*, ed. Robert S. Siegler (New York: L. Erlbaum Associates, 1978).

children's *knowledge base* of the game of chess allowed them to outperform the grown-ups in that chess-related task.[107]

Our lesson here is that a sizable knowledge base of both important ethical principles and factual information about the kinds of tasks and situations in which we are placed will make it far easier for us to make quick, wise decisions when faced with the unexpected. If we are to think well on our feet, our feet need to be planted on a firm, substantial knowledge base.[108]

Further, there is good news at the opposite end of the life span as well, for although various mental capacities (such as those for retaining new learning, mental quickness at recall and calculations, and so forth) may show some decline, one's knowledge base, as measured by things such as retention of long-known facts and vocabulary, tend to remain very robust even in healthy individuals who are very elderly.

And one last point about the value of a broad, firm knowledge base. Often, and as recently as last week, I've seen it argued that we don't need to memorize things or build a vast knowledge base

---

[107] In a very interesting twist, later research showed that when the chess pieces were arranged in patterns that would not be possible in an actual game, the children did not recall them as well. Their knowledge base was not as relevant to that memory task.

[108] In a recent talk I gave on memory techniques, a member of the audience asked if I thought that in modern educational methods there was too much focus on "critical thinking" (analyzing and breaking down issues and finding flaws in arguments) at the expense of memorization and acquiring a broad knowledge base. I said I thought it was good for students to be adept at critical thinking — if they have also learned things worth critically thinking about. After all, it is hard to think critically about things that one does not know and understand!

because the answer to virtually any factual question can be found on our computers or in those amazing little smart phones that fit in the palms of our hands.

To those who think that way, I offer this question: If you required an important invasive surgery, who would you prefer to operate on you: the world's most knowledgeable computer expert in an operating room surrounded by the world's most powerful computers, or an average, run-of-the mill surgeon? Surely, the IT man would have virtually all the recorded medical knowledge gathered throughout the history of man, accessible with merely a click of his fingers or even an audible question. The surgeon would have rapid access to far less medical knowledge. The crucial difference, of course, is that the surgeon's knowledge base lies *in his head*—and hands! It has become internalized. I don't know about you, but I'd choose him. Now, if it came to a computer issue, of course we would choose our world's greatest IT man, because in that realm, through his own years of training and practice, he, too, has acquired a vast knowledge base that is in his head and hands. It is certainly good to know how to access information from outside sources, but it is prudent to know that there is much knowledge worth learning and storing between our two ears, information relevant not only to our professional lives but to our spiritual lives as well.

### On Grounding Our Knowledge Base
### on the Ground of All Being

An understanding of the things of God should serve as the foundation and the peak of our knowledge base, with knowledge of Christ as the "cornerstone" of its edifice (1 Pet. 2:6) and "the rock" (1 Cor. 10:4) that holds it together and strengthens it. Such knowledge of Scripture and Church teaching was clearly the foundation and the summit of St. Thomas's learning. If you read virtually any page of the *Summa Theologica*, for example (and I pray that you will), you will find a plethora of scriptural quotations and the teachings of Church Doctors. If you read its very first question (article 5), you will find that Thomas called theology "sacred doctrine," the "noblest" of all sciences, citing both Scripture ("Wisdom sent her maids to invite to the tower" [Prov. 9:3]) and Aristotle, who wrote in his *de Animalibus* (On Animals) that even "the slenderest knowledge that may be obtained of the highest things is more desirable than the most certain knowledge obtained of lesser things." The wisdom God reveals to us is the ultimate and highest wisdom, which makes sense of and gives meaning to all the other knowledge we obtain through the "handmaids" that serve it. (And this is not at all to denigrate, but to elevate, the value of those handmaids themselves, a few of which we'll highlight shortly.)

God is the source and the summit of all knowledge and truth, and any time we use our thinking powers to obtain the truth, we are seeking some reflection of the beauty and goodness of the One who is the Truth. Still, we seek His truths most directly when we devote time to study the truths He revealed to us in Scripture and the insights and interpretations produced by the Church He bequeathed to us while on earth. So then, we need to apply our powers of memory, of understanding, and of study to the things of God on a regular basis, and if we thus become suffused with God's word, the thinking we do on our feet will be ever more prudent, and even those feet, so to speak, will be ever more blessed and beautiful (see Isa. 52:7; Rom. 10:15)!

We should, of course, set aside some time on a regular basis for study of the Scriptures, the *Catechism of the Catholic Church*, the *Summa Theologica*, other writings of the saints, and the documents and activities (such as the sacred liturgy of the Mass) that comprise Catholic Tradition. But what else? What are some worthwhile "handmaidens," other fields of knowledge truly worthy of study for the modern Catholic who would think like Aquinas? What other kinds of reading should we undertake in a lifelong pursuit of a general self-education conducive to real intellectual and spiritual growth? I'd like to suggest three broad areas of study that can help us think like Aquinas.

*History*

The study of history can provide a great and powerful knowledge blast from the past. Catholics would be wise to acquaint themselves with the richness of Church history, from the fascinating *Church History* of Eusebius (263–339), "the Father of Church History," through the historical works of twentieth-century literary giants G. K. Chesterton and Hilaire Belloc, to the books of so many good Catholic historians still writing today. Secular histories and biographies, too, can serve to build our knowledge base of important truths about human nature, politics, war, and so much more. "Those who don't remember the past are condemned to repeat it," goes a saying attributed to eighteenth-century political philosopher Edmund Burke. Surely, part of the reason Thomas made so few mistakes in philosophy and theology is that he was so steeped in their histories.

*Philosophy*

Philosophy is the *philos* (love) of *sophia* (wisdom), and Thomas loved philosophy like few others before or since. Thomas's philosophical knowledge base was built out of the solid bricks of Aristotle's philosophy more than any others, but he knew well and profited from the philosophy of Plato, Cicero, Seneca, and many others. In fact, he used their ideas abundantly and cited them repeatedly in the *Summa Theologica* and in many other works. For readers not inclined to study the deep mysteries of metaphysics or the rigorous rules of logic, some of the most practical and useful of ancient philosophical ideas can be found in their works on practical ethics and virtues. There are many valuable lessons waiting there for modern Catholics, just as there were for the harvesting by St. Thomas Aquinas and other great theologians and Church Fathers. Among the most accessible and enjoyable works you can read to build your philosophical knowledge base are Aristotle's *Nicomachean Ethics* (about which Thomas wrote his own masterful commentary on every single line!), Cicero's *On Duties*, Seneca's *Letters* and *Moral Essays*, Epictetus's *Handbook* and *Discourses*, and Emperor Marcus Aurelius' famous *Meditations*.

*Literature*
Whereas history tells us what people have done, literature can inspire us about what we might do. Great works of literature represent the powers of the imagination and hypothetical reasoning at their most magnificent. Great books spanning diverse historical eras and locales can expand our knowledge base in profoundly moving ways. The best of these books will stir our emotions to feel compassion toward others and to achieve worthwhile goals and relationships. We saw earlier that both Sts. Thomas and John the Evangelist recommend refreshing periods of play interspersed with periods of diligent study. Modern psychologists also speak of the value of the Premack Principle (referred to by some as "Grandma's law"): "First you work, and then you play." In other words, we can increase our tendency to do hard things (such as study) if we reward study periods with pleasures, such as relaxation or play.

The pleasures produced by some great works of literature allow us, in a sense, to *play while we work!* And indeed, there are times when St. Thomas, like St. Paul before him, cites classical literary works in his writings.

---

## Doctor's Orders ✍️

*Prescription for Filling Your Mental Cupboard with Scads of Savory Truths*

### Reflect

Did anything in this chapter hit home with you? Are there any significant gaps in your education or cracks in the foundation of your knowledge base that you need to fill? Are there any personal peaks that you might raise yet higher? Have you formulated a study plan to grow your knowledge base? Is your "cell" ready now, and have you charted out a time or times of day when you can regularly get down to business?[109]

### Read

I'll forgo the formal "read" prescription, since many possible recommendations were made within the chapter. I will note that Thomas addresses the virtue of *solertia*, or shrewdness, in his *Summa Theologica*.[110] While *docility*, as we saw in chapter 1, is the virtue through which we dispose ourselves toward learning

---

[109] Thomas's study habits included prayer, celebration of Mass and attendance at another Mass, teaching, and theological and philosophical reading and writing virtually all day, every day, and well into the night. What does— or will— *your* daily routine look like?

[110] *Summa Theologica*, II-II, Q. 49, art. 4.

from others, shrewdness is the capacity to think quickly on our own two feet. The more knowledge we have made our own and internalized through study, the more mental resources we will have available to make swift, accurate decisions when there's no time to seek advice from others. I'll also note here the power of *rereading* again and again worthwhile books, foremost among them Scripture. Not only is repetition the mother of memory, but sometimes lessons that fly over our heads will get through to our gray matter years down the road, when our experiences have opened our minds and hearts to grasp the truths of those lessons better and to apply them swiftly and prudently in our circumstances. In the words of Shakespeare's *King Lear*, "ripeness is all."

### Remember

Have you internalized the gist of the first nine precepts? If not, just take another mental walk around the first nine places in our mnemonic foyer.

*Chapter 10*

# Knowing Your Mental
# Powers — and Their Limits

*Seek not the things that are too high for thee.*

### How High Is Too High for You — at This Time?

Thomas quotes Sirach in this piece of counsel.[111] We would be amiss to interpret it as advice *not* to seek understanding of the highest and most important things of God, because to do so would be to neglect the "for thee." We are to seek the highest truths we are capable of grasping. This will vary from person to person and, more importantly, even in ourselves over time. Here, Thomas prepares to conclude his brief letter by reinforcing his early advice to seek out the vast sea first through the means of navigable rivers. A parallel verse in Sirach is "Do not lift a weight beyond your strength" (13:2), and every weightlifter knows well that with proper, diligent training over time, the weight that is beyond your strength today may become like child's play at some point in the future. We are to seek the highest truths, but not in so great a hurry that we fail to build within ourselves the strength

---

[111] Sir. 3:21: "Seek not what is too difficult for you" in the RSVCE.

of mind to grasp and hold on to them. In the spirit of docility, we will also heed our trainers' guidance, so that when those who have already attained the heights reach down to offer us a hand, we will not fail to clasp it with gratitude. We will also bear in mind that some of the most glorious truths of the Catholic Faith, including the Trinity and the Incarnation, are *mysteries* that surpass the limitations of any human's understanding.

### *"Lift No Weight Beyond Your Strength" — for Now*

Speaking of Sirach's sage advice not to exceed our intellectual, spiritual, or physical strength, we'd be wise to keep in mind that all of our capacities can be enhanced within limits. Recall, if you will, Thomas's maxims that art perfects nature, and grace perfects them both. Further, as soul-body unities, we can improve our mental powers by improving our physical health, for as the ancient Greeks and Romans knew well, a healthy mind thrives best within a healthy body.

Thomas wrote that "virtue, inasmuch as it is a suitable disposition of the soul, is like health and beauty, which are suitable dispositions of the body."[112] Further, he noted, commenting on Aristotle, that "to a good bodily disposition corresponds the nobility of the soul."[113]

To think most effectively then, we must take care of the health of our bodies. Father Sertillanges, whose great work *The Intellectual Life* also drew from St. Thomas's letter on study, was very explicit in his exercise recommendations to any person who would seek to perfect his intellect. He said we should always strive to stay well, and he particularly recommended walking after the

---

[112] *Summa Theologica*, I-II, Q. 55, art. 2.
[113] Cited in Sertillanges and Ryan, *The Intellectual Life*, 33.

fashion of the ancient Greeks. Of course, St. Thomas honored one of those Greeks with the title "the Philosopher,"[114] and his school happened to be known as the Peripatetics, those who walk about, because of the colonnaded walkways of his school, the Lyceum, where the students would walk around. According to some legends, Aristotle himself lectured as he walked! Further, Dominicans in Thomas's day generally traversed Europe on foot, and Thomas himself was known to walk while immersed in deep thought.

In any event, Father Sertillanges recommended daily walking, stretching, and moving in the open air, if possible. Further, for those who could not get out, he recommended some "excellent substitute methods" calling those of J. P. Muller "one of the most intelligent." Jorgen Peter Muller (1866–1938) was a gymnastics instructor and health educator who advocated brief (fifteen-minute) daily sessions of bodyweight exercises and stretching movements, a forerunner of the brief but intense High Intensity Training methods that I use and advocate.[115]

So then, these important mind-body connections were well known to the Greeks of the fourth century B.C., to St. Thomas of the thirteenth century, and to Father Sertillanges of the nineteenth century. But it has been primarily only near the end of the twentieth and the beginning of the twenty-first century that scientific data showing just *how* and *why* exercise enhances our ability to think has steadily mounted. I first heard of this research

---

[114] And Thomas was not alone in this. St. Albert the Great and St. Bonaventure were among others who gave Aristotle that title.

[115] See Kevin Vost, *Fit for Eternal Life: A Christian Approach to Working Out, Eating Right, and Building the Virtues of Fitness in Your Soul* (Manchester, NH: Sophia Institute Press, 2007).

when talking to a business professor at, of all places, Aquinas College in Nashville, Tennessee, when he brought to my attention the work of psychiatrist John J. Ratey, M.D.[116]

## *Firing Your Brain's Spark Plugs*

Dr. Ratey, the author of *Spark: The Revolutionary New Science of Exercise and the Brain*,[117] has boldly declared: "Exercise is the single most powerful tool you have to optimize your brain function."[118] He bases his claim upon a vast, growing body of experimental research studies in recent decades from around the world, using both animal and human subjects, that links various forms of aerobic and strength-training regimens to enhanced levels of a variety of neurotransmitters, such as dopamine, gamma-aminobutyric acid (GABA), glutamate, norepinephrine, and serotonin, and proteins and hormones such as brain-derived neurotrophic factor (BDNF), fibroblast growth factor (FGF-2), human growth hormone (HGH),[119] insulin-like growth factor 1 (IGF-1), and vascu-

---

[116] Thank you, Dr. Dan Donnelly!

[117] John J. Ratey and Eric Hagerman, *Spark: The Revolutionary New Science of Exercise and the Brain* (New York: Little, Brown, 2008).

[118] Marie Snider, "Miracle-Gro for Brains," *Exercise Revolution* (blog), March 2008, http://johnratey.typepad.com/blog/2008/03/miracle-gro-for.html.

[119] HGH production has been found to be stimulated most strongly by intense exercises using the body's biggest muscles, so that, for example, short intense sprints stimulate more than walking or jogging. To my pleasant surprise—though, it really should not have been surprising—Dr. Ratey notes that the greatest HGH response has been found in response to intense barbell squats (weighted deep-knee bends) that involve several of the body's biggest and strongest muscles in unison. Strength trainers have been aware for many decades that exercises such as squats best

lar endothelial growth factor (VEGF), which help form and grow synaptic connections between brain cells and promote growth and regeneration of brain cells themselves. Some studies have shown measurable growth in particular brain structures in response to exercise—for example, growth in the hippocampus in schizophrenics who rode exercise bikes, and growth in brain volume in the frontal and temporal lobes in sixty- to seventy-nine-year-olds who walked on a treadmill thrice weekly for six months.

Further, many studies have found, in addition to positive changes in *body chemicals* and *structures*, significant changes in response to regular exercise in *actual cognitive functioning* in terms of outcomes such as improved standardized-testing scores among high school students who underwent regulated, progressive aerobic conditioning during PE classes and 20 percent improvement in vocabulary learning among adults immediately following an exercise session.

Although it is difficult to think clearly and learn new information while performing demanding exercise because of the increased demand on blood flow to the working muscles, the hormonal and chemical changes stimulated by exercise produce both short-term and long-term benefits in thinking capacities afterward, because of the positive changes in the neurological and cardiovascular systems that feed needed nutrients to the brain. Further, milder forms of exercise, such as walking at a leisurely pace, often enhance our thinking abilities even while we are doing them.

There are yet other ways in which exercise can help improve our thinking that highlight Aristotle's and St. Thomas's

---

stimulate overall muscle growth and size, but did not know the chemical mechanisms behind it.

insights into the parallels between bodily health and virtues of the soul. Thomas emphasized something that perhaps we have all experienced: the clouding of clear thought by uncontrolled passions such as lust or anger. That is why, although prudence directs moral virtues such as temperance or self-control and patience, it also depends on them to control the kinds of passions that impair our practical reasoning abilities. Exercise can operate in a similar way to regulate some emotions that can impair our ability to think effectively. Ratey includes chapters on the beneficial effects of exercise on problems such as anxiety, depression, attention deficit disorders, and addictions—because of the cascade of positive chemical changes that exercise can stimulate in the brain and other parts of the body, thereby impacting the mind.

Along with my previous specialization in Alzheimer's dementia, another area of particular interest to me was the potential impact of exercise on the onset and severity of it. Even in my doctoral training days in the 1990s, while there was certainly no guaranteed method of avoiding dementia, the widely recommended rule was "use it or lose it," meaning that the research suggested that those who remained most active, *both physically and mentally*, were less likely to become demented in old age.

My own training and research into aging and cognition was completed with the aid of elderly Dominican, Franciscan, and Ursuline sisters who had volunteered for a study through the Southern Illinois University School of Medicine. (I narrowly missed the chance to test my fourth-grade teacher, who once gave me a D in conduct, but that's another story.) Many of the sisters remained very sharp well into their ninth decade. (The first person to repeat back to me a list of fifteen words *in their exact order* after several trials was a retired Ursuline teacher in her late eighties!) Other groups of religious sisters throughout the United States have volunteered and helped us learn more about brain functioning and dementia.

Dr. Ratey tells the interesting story of a Sister Bernadette of the School Sisters of Notre Dame in Mankato, Minnesota. Right up until the time she died of a heart attack in the 1990s, she scored in the top 10 percent of her age group in tests of cognitive abilities such as memory, language, and visual-spatial abilities. She donated her brain to science, and most surprisingly, after death, her hippocampus was found to be full of the plaques and tangles characteristic of the damage wrought by Alzheimer's disease, despite the fact that her cognitive capacities had remained superb! Researchers speculated that because she stayed so mentally active, she developed cognitive reserve capacity in response to the damage. Healthy brain tissue was likely recruited to help maintain cognitive function through different routes, which sounds to me quite akin to the phenomenon of "collateral circulation" protecting the heart, wherein minor blood vessels enlarge to enhance circulation to compensate for damage to large vessels, a process that may be aided by physical exercise.

So, what is the bottom line for those who would like to maximize the health of their bodies and brains to keep thinking more like Aquinas? Dr. Ratey recommends that every healthy person[120] exercise regularly and that anyone *over sixty* should exercise almost every day. He recommends two strength-training sessions and four mild to moderate aerobic sessions (walking, jogging, biking, cardio machines, and so forth) every week.

---

[120] Anyone starting or significantly changing an exercise program should consult his physician first to rule out any existing conditions that could make exercise dangerous.

Exercise can be powerful medicine even in small doses. A minimal, but effective regimen could entail as little as *one* brief (twenty- to thirty-minute) strength workout (free weights, machines, or body weight exercises) and *three* brief (twenty- to thirty-minute) aerobic workouts (walking, running, swimming, and so forth) or vigorous sessions of normal house and yard work.[121]

### *Practice Intellectual Humility, but Not Pusillanimity!*

In encouraging Brother John (and all of us) not to seek things too high for us, Thomas endorses intellectual *humility*. The word "humility" comes from the Latin *humus*, for "ground, earth, or soil." When we are humble, we remember that we are indeed "ashes to ashes, dust to dust," as we are reminded on Ash Wednesday and at funeral services (see Gen. 3:19). Which one of us gave ourselves our own existence? As Christ proclaimed to St. Catherine of Siena in a mystical ecstasy:

"Do you know, daughter, who you are, and who I am? If you know these two things, you will be blessed. You are she who is not; whereas I am He who is."[122]

In practicing intellectual humility, we always remember the limits of our human powers of understanding. All of our human knowledge begins with the things of this earth, and what our senses reveal to us about them. God has graced us with intellectual

---

[121] The manner in which strength training is performed is very important, especially for its safe and effective performance by the elderly. There is a chapter on their needs in *Fit for Eternal Life*.

[122] Blessed Raymond of Capua, *The Life of St. Catherine of Siena* (Charlotte, NC: St. Benedict Press, 2006), 62. Cf. Exod. 3:14.

powers, but great mysteries of the Faith, such as the Holy Trinity, will always exceed our powers to grasp them fully. Nonetheless, we should never confuse the lofty virtue of *humility* with the lowly vice of *pusillanimity*.

"Pusillanimity" derives from the Latin word *pusillus*, meaning "very little, petty, or paltry." In the words of St. Thomas Aquinas:

> Pusillanimity makes a man fall short of what is proportionate to his power.... Hence it is that the servant who buried in the earth the money that he received from his master, and did not trade with it through fainthearted fear, was punished by his master.[123]

The second half of the word "-animity" refers to the *anima* — Latin for "soul." To be pusillanimous, then, is to be "small souled," and this is not what God wants of us. Recalling the parable of the talents, which Thomas cited (Matt. 25:14–30), God, our most generous Master, is most pleased when we take whatever talents He gives us and multiply them to the utmost of our abilities for His honor and glory.

God calls us to be humble in remembering our lowly origins and limited abilities, but He does not call us to the vice of pusillanimity. Rather, He invites us to build and share its direct opposite, the virtue of *magnanimity* — true *magna* (greatness) of soul. While humility rightly recognizes the limits of our innate humanity, magnanimity recalls that we can do all things "through Christ who strengthens us" (see Phil. 4:13).

St. Thomas masterfully dispels the paradox of a conflict between magnanimity and humility by calling to our attention both the divine and the natural elements of our humanity. We are

---

[123] *Summa Theologica*, II-II, Q. 133, art. 1.

given great and powerful gifts from God, such as the intellectual powers this book is all about! We also have a sinful, fallen human nature. Magnanimity reflects our consideration of that divine spark within us, the recognition that we are greatly blessed by God and should use our powers for the greatest works of good within our capacities. "Be perfect as your heavenly Father is perfect," said Jesus (Matt. 5:48).

Magnanimity reflects this striving for perfection. Humility reflects the recognition of that weaker, sinful side of our nature. It recognizes that, although we must always strive to do great things and to make ourselves perfect, we never fully achieve that state in this life. Further, when we express the virtue of humility, we recognize the *greatness of soul* that God has also provided *in our neighbor*. The truly magnanimous person, then, strives for great and honorable things and also wishes the same for his neighbor. He strives for truths within reach, recognizes the limits of that reach, and tries to stretch it with God's grace and to help his neighbor reach yet higher too.

---

## Doctor's Orders

*Prescription for Knowing Your Limits (and Stretching Them)*

### Reflect

Might you take a few minutes to consider what habits of diet, exercise, rest, prayer, or study either help or hinder your abilities to make the most of your God-given powers of thought, and then make prudent efforts to weed out the bad dispositions and tendencies and replace them with virtuous ones? Have you reflected on how you might grow both in the humility that grounds us and the magnanimity that raises us?

**Read**

In his *Summa*, Thomas writes about humility in the context of its relationship to the virtue of temperance[124] and writes about magnanimity and pusillanimity in the context of their relationship to the virtue of fortitude.[125] For more information on both the scientific research on the positive effects of exercise on thinking capacities, and practical recommendations on what kind and how much exercise to do, see Dr. John Ratey's *Spark: The Revolutionary New Science of Exercise and the Brain* and the amazingly vigorous octogenarian fitness expert Clarence Bass's *Take Charge: Fitness at the Edge of Science*.[126] The book that best explains the many benefits of proper strength training and the briefest and safest ways to obtain them is *Body by Science*, by emergency-room physician Doug McGuff, M.D.[127] Father Sertillanges's recommendations on exercise for the intellectual can be found in his *Intellectual Life*, chapter 2 on "The Virtues of a Catholic Intellectual," section 4, on "The Discipline of the Body." My own look at the relationship between fitness and virtue can be found in *Fit for Eternal Life: A Christian Approach to Working Out, Eating Right, and Building the Virtues of Fitness in Your Soul* and in my devotional with co-authors Peggy Bowes

---

[124] *Summa Theologica*, II-II. Q. 161.

[125] Ibid., II-II, Q. 129 and 133.

[126] Clarence Bass and Carol Bass, *Take Charge: Fitness at the Edge of Science* (Albuquerque, NM: Clarence Bass' Ripped Enterprises, 2013).

[127] Doug McGuff and John R. Little, *Body by Science: A Research Based Program for Strength Training, Body Building, and Complete Fitness in 12 Minutes a Week* (New York: McGraw-Hill, 2009).

and Shane Kapler, *Tending the Temple: 365 Days of Spiritual and Physical Devotions*.[128]

### Remember

Have you internalized the gist of all ten precepts now? If not, take another mental walk around the first nine places in our mnemonic foyer. Are they stored safe and sound in your treasure chest of memory? In part 2 you'll come to know like the back of your hand the rest of this house and its intriguing contents, all designed to help you think more like Aquinas.

---

[128] Kevin Vost, Shane Kapler, and Peggy Bowes, *Tending the Temple* (Waterford, MI: Bezalel Books, 2011).

# Conclusion to Part 1

*Follow in the footsteps of blessed Dominic, who brought forth useful and wonderful leaves, flowers, and fruits in the vineyard of the Lord of Hosts for as long as life was his fellow traveler. If you shall have followed these steps, you will be able to attain whatever you desire. Farewell!*

## *Following the Founder's Footsteps in the Vineyard of the Lord*

Thomas ends by advising Brother John to follow in the footsteps of St. Dominic de Guzman (1170–1221), the founder of their Order of Preachers. Although this is the only direct reference to Dominic in Thomas's extant writings, Dominic's impact on Thomas's thought and life was clearly immense. Dominic founded their order to bring the truth of Christ's gospel to the Cathars in Southern France who had been taken in by the Albigensian heresy, a variation of age-old Manichean ideas that saw the material world (including the body) as evil, and only the realm of the spirit as good.[129] Dominic knew well the Church's position that all of God's creation was good (see Gen. 1:4, 10,

---

[129] See chapter 13 for details on these heresies.

12, 18, 21, 25, 31). He knew that to convert the Cathars, and later the whole world, to the truth, his preachers needed to know the truth, so *Veritas* (Truth) became one of his religious order's early mottos. For this reason, *study* itself became a hallmark and one of the "four pillars" of the Dominican Order.[130]

Further, in keeping with Thomas's advice to Brother John on study as a "way of life," Dominic knew that sinners and heretics would be converted not merely by abstract truths but through *the example of those who preached to them.* He knew that where rich and powerful bishops and abbots, with all their fine vestments, horses, and retinues, had failed to reach the heretics who believed they were true to Christ's humble example, his friars and brothers who embraced poverty, chastity, and obedience would help win their hearts as well as their minds. To be a Dominican was to follow and to proclaim Christ, the "way, the truth, and the life." Thomas reminds Brother John, then, of his calling as a Dominican, and yet one need not be a professed Dominican to share in their bountiful lessons.

Christ told us that He is the vine, and we are the branches, and that we should bear abiding fruit (see John 15:5, 16). Dominic was a branch who so followed Christ that his leaves, flowers, and fruits still abide and nourish us in our world today. Thomas tells Brother John (and us as well) the good news that if we follow Dominic's example, as he followed Christ's, paying heed to all the precepts in this little study guide, we will acquire *quidquid affectus* — whatever we desire![131] This is possible when our study

---

[130] As we noted earlier, the other three pillars are *preaching, prayer,* and *community.*

[131] I can't help but observe the parallel with the language Thomas used when visited by Sts. Peter and Paul, as we saw in chapter 6.

is founded in prayer and grounded in Christ, for Christ told us "with God all things are possible" (Matt. 19:26).

### *Unleashing All Your Intellectual Powers*

As we come to the end of part 1, I get my last chance to drive some thoughts home. So, let's buckle up and begin.

First of all, I hope you have come to see, through the wisdom of St. Thomas Aquinas, how your capacities to think, study, and make prudent decisions in your life are truly wonderful intellectual *powers*, given to you by God. God has given each one of us a potentially powerful intellect and it is up to us whether we choose to open up the throttle of its sundry powers or just sit there idling. God is not pleased with the inaction of the lukewarm (Rev. 3:16), with those who would bury their talents under the ground (Matt. 25:24–30) or hide their lights under a bushel basket (Matt. 5:15).[132] Indeed, He calls us to be perfect (Matt. 5:48), making the most of all the gifts He has given us, showing our gratitude to Him, and sharing the fruits of our powers with others.

Virtues such as docility, studiousness, prudence, and magnanimity are the oars with which we row into ever broader streams of knowledge. The gifts of the Holy Spirit, such as knowledge, understanding, and wisdom, are the powerful winds behind us, if we but unfurl our sails!

---

Thomas told Brother Reginald that they "told me all I desired to know."

[132] That St. Thomas embodies the polar opposite of hiding one's light under a basket can be seen from one of the symbols the Church has bestowed upon him, that of a blazing sun on his chest, representing the way he illuminates us to this day. (Such a statue sits to my left on my desk, inspiring me as I write.)

Hopefully, Thomas has enlightened us with a greater understanding of the intellectual powers that we may not have realized we have, and inflamed our hearts with zeal to practice and perfect our powers of thinking, and to improve our lives and the lives of our neighbors as we and they grow in happiness and in holiness.

### From Half-Truths to Wholes

Thomas wrote at great length about *justice*, and he always strove after the same thing sought out by our courts of law: "the truth, the whole truth, and nothing but the truth." Hopefully, that will be another unforgettable message from these pages. The world as a whole does not think like Aquinas and threatens to smother us with half-digested half-truths. Our culture often asks us to choose either faith or reason, science or religion, cherished principles or tolerance, tradition or progress, pleasure or virtue, and to respond to many more false either-or dichotomies. Thomas answers that we are made to seek *both* in their right measure, using the powers of our minds to look at all sides of important issues, ferreting out little truths wherever they may be found, so that we may attain the *fullness of truth* within our capacities to know it.

St. Thomas can help us transcend yet another crucial false dichotomy of our day, one that says we must choose to guide our lives by the cool *reasoning* of the rational mind *or* the warm fires of heartfelt *emotion*. Thomas chose *both* the head and the heart, both warm wisdom and loving, burning charity. Reginald of Piperno, Thomas's confessor and closest friend of his last years of life, noted that "very often, during Mass, he burst into tears. Sometimes the congregation witnessed it." Those who would think like Aquinas will strive to love like him, too, seeking to know God better, so as to love Him more deeply.

St. Thomas was the world's greatest synthesizer and integrator of truths. He should inspire us to try to do likewise, within the limits of our powers, as he reminds us in his last precept.

## From Thoughts to Deeds

We need to train ourselves, then, to *think* like Aquinas in seeking the fullness of *truth* so that we may better *act* like him too, executing the kind of prudent actions in our lives that will help us attain the *ultimate end* of the *goodness* of God. St. Thomas knew well that "faith, by itself, if it has not works, is dead" (James 2:17). Let thinking like Aquinas strengthen in us a faith that works!

## Through Him, with Him, and in Him

At the beginning of his academic career, young Thomas chose to give his first lecture at the University of Paris in 1256, expounding on this scriptural verse: "From your heights you water the mountains; the earth is filled with the fruits of your works" (Ps. 103:13, Douay-Rheims). Water comes to the mountains from the heavens above, forming rivers that flow down to the earth, giving it life and making it fertile. "Similarly, the minds of teachers, symbolized by the mountains, are watered by the things that are above in the wisdom of God, and by their ministry the light of divine wisdom flows down into the minds of students."[133]

Those mountainous minds of whom Thomas speaks are the teachers of Sacred Scripture who need to be "high" in the quality of their lives, so that they, like the prophets and apostles before them, will be able to pass on to others the life-giving rains of

---

[133] Cited in Simon Tugwell, ed., *Albert and Thomas: Selected Writings* (New York: Paulist Press, 1988), 355.

God's wisdom. So ardently did this young professor respect and ascend to those mountains of wisdom that he himself finally came to be among the loftiest of all peaks. To this day, He sends down divine rivers of wisdom that nourish hearts and minds.

Not even two decades passed from the day of that lecture to the time when Thomas had produced a veritable Everest of wisdom in the millions of words that his multitudinous commentaries and *Summas* comprise. May he inspire every one of us, regardless of our abilities or calling in life, to strive to bring all our thinking into the service of Jesus Christ by thinking more like Aquinas!

Near the end of his life, as he knelt before a crucifix, St. Thomas experienced a vision of Christ. When Christ told Thomas that he had written well about Him and asked Thomas what reward he desired, Thomas's answer was "*Non nisi Te*" (None but You, Lord).

Might we all come to think like Aquinas!

# Fathoming the Depths of Wisdom

# Prologue to Part 2

*Lastly, another crown seems to have been kept for this peerless man—that is, the way in which he extorts homage, praise, and admiration from the enemies of the Catholic name.*

—Pope Leo XIII on St. Thomas Aquinas, *Aeterni Patris*

*Catholicism had once been the most philosophical of all religions. Its long, illustrious philosophical history was illuminated by a giant: Thomas Aquinas. He brought an Aristotelian view of reason (an Aristotelian epistemology) back into European culture, and lighted the way to the Renaissance. For the brief span of the nineteenth century, when his was the dominant influence among Catholic philosophers, the grandeur of his thought almost lifted the Church close to the realm of reason.*

—Ayn Rand (self-proclaimed "greatest enemy of religion"), "Requiem for Man," *Capitalism*

## The Practical Wisdom of Reason Seeking God

Prudence entails choosing the right means to attain the right ends, and here St. Thomas was sublimely prudent, for his means were both reason and faith to attain the ends of both fleeting earthly happiness and, far more important, eternal bliss. Not all who profess faith in Christ duly respect our God-given capacities of reason,[134] but St. Thomas did, like few others before or since. It is because of this great respect for the truths that can be derived from human reason that some, though certainly not all, enemies of the Catholic Church still acknowledge his great contributions to human knowledge. Indeed, our quotation from atheist philosopher Ayn Rand was penned decades *after* the one from Pope Leo XIII, and the era of the nineteenth century she wrote about was the time during which Leo strove mightily to "spread the golden wisdom of St. Thomas Aquinas."

Rand, unlike Thomas, did not acknowledge the ultimate compatibility of faith and reason; hence her less-than-flattering conclusion that the Church was "almost" lifted "close to the realm of reason." Still, reason can provide the common starting ground for discussion between Christians and atheists or agnostics who do not acknowledge the authority of Scripture and the Church. Indeed, Pope Leo would write that the writings of the Church Fathers and Scholastic philosophers and theologians (St. Thomas foremost among them) would be the most likely means to draw into the Catholic Faith people who had come to respect reason alone (and indeed, it happened just like that to me!).

Decades ago, I stumbled across a most unusual and surprising tribute both to the power of reason to draw people to the Faith and to the powerful example of St. Thomas Aquinas. Yesterday, I reread it. There, in a collection of what was voted by science fiction writers as the twenty-six best science fiction short stories of all time (up to its first publication in 1970), I found "The Quest for Saint Aquin" by Anthony Boucher, penned in 1951.

---

[134] See "Fideism" in chapter 12.

To make a short story shorter, in a futuristic world, post nuclear holocaust, the government is run by technocrats, and Christianity has been outlawed. Believers, priests, and the pope himself must conceal their identities, much like the early Christians in Rome, who secretly met in houses or in the catacombs and communicated their shared belief through subtle symbols. The pope hears stories of a powerful saintly man named Aquin who had converted many to the Church through the matchless power of his logic. His body is rumored to lie incorrupt in a secluded mountain cave not far away. The pope sends a priest named Thomas to investigate, transported there by an intelligent, speaking robotic donkey with legs as well as wheels, since the roads had so deteriorated.

A little theological discussion ensues on the way, and the robotic donkey declares to Father Thomas that it has a perfectly programmed logical mind that cannot make the error of believing in God.

When they find the apparently incorrupt body of Aquin, the robotic donkey crushes the skin on one of his hands and reveals to Father Thomas that the "saint" was actually a *robot*! The robotic donkey encourages him to report to the pope that they found the incorrupt saint, since his mission is to draw people into the Church through such miracles. Father Thomas, however, refuses to do so, declaring, "Faith cannot be based on a lie," and here is where his insights get quite interesting:

> "Now I understand the name of Aquin," he went on to himself. "We've known of Thomas Aquinas, the Angelic Doctor, the perfect reasoner of the church. His writings are lost, but surely somewhere in the world we can find a copy. We can train our young men to develop his

reasoning still further. We have trusted too long in faith alone; this is not an age of faith. We must call reason into our service — and Aquin has shown us that perfect reason can lead only to God."[135]

As the story goes, the robot Aquin truly had been programmed with perfect logical reasoning capacities. It knew that it had been built by man but reasoned that man, its maker, could not have made himself and must have been created by God. Therefore, deducing that his duties lay to man, his maker, and to his maker's Maker, the robot Aquin spent all his energies converting people through unassailable logic to belief in God and the Catholic Church!

As for the actual arguments of St. Thomas of Aquinas that lead inevitably to confirm God's existence and essential attributes (e.g., oneness, changelessness, omniscience, omnipotence, eternity), they are especially powerful because they start with simple observations available to anyone and they point to the necessity of God's existence, *even if* we grant the point to some philosophers that the universe always existed. Thomas knew from revelation that God *created* the universe, but he believed that reason alone could not decide the matter. Aristotle, for example, believed that the universe always existed, but he also believed that reason proved that God must exist to *sustain* it.

St. Thomas's arguments are, in logical terminology, *a posteriori*, based on observable facts, rather than *a priori*, beginning

---

[135] Anthony Boucher, "The Quest for Saint Aquin," in *Science Fiction Hall of Fame*, ed. Lester del Rey (New York: Avon, 1971), 475.

with theoretical assumptions.[136] He goes on briefly in the *Summa Theologica* to lay out five arguments based on things that are evident to our senses when we look at the world. By the observations that (1) things move or change, having as yet unactualized potentials, (2) there are effects and causes, (3) things exist for a time and then perish, (4) there are varying degrees of goodness or perfection in things, and (5) there is ordered or purposeful behavior in nature, Thomas shows that there must exist (1) a first or unmoved mover that is completely actualized and unchanging, (2) a first or uncaused cause, (3) a necessary being that cannot *not* exist, (4) a perfection of being from which lesser degrees of goodness flow, and (5) a first and final cause that provides for the order and governance of the entire universe.

Bearing in mind that he grants the concession for argument's sake that the universe always existed, you will see that his arguments are not dependent (as many modern critics suppose) merely on time and do not require a chronological regression. The great chains of causation, perfection, order, and purpose require a prime mover, a first efficient cause, a necessary being, an ultimate formal cause, and a final cause for their existence, not merely sometime in the past, but *at this very moment and at every moment.* "We live and move and have our being" (Acts 17:28) right now through the grace, love, and power of an eternal God.

Reason functions at its highest level when it leads us to the God who created us and sustains us, but it also has many

---

[136] This *a posteriori* approach (reasoning from the facts of the world to the existence of God) is found in Scripture. See, for example, Romans 1:20: "Ever since the creation of the world his [God's] invisible nature, namely, his eternal power and deity, has been clearly perceived in the things that have been made."

additional useful functions in God's service in the practical acts of our daily lives, which is the stuff of the virtue of prudence. Before we examine examples of how reason can be led astray through logical fallacies in chapter 11, let's take a logical and reasonable preliminary step by looking at logic and reason themselves.

### Being Logical, Practical (but Not Clinical, Cynical, Fanatical, Radical)

If you are as old as I am, you will remember "The Logical Song," by the band Supertramp from the 1970s. Here the singer laments how he was taught to be "logical, practical, clinical, and cynical" and more at school, but he is left with a burning question and pleads "Please tell me who I am." G. K. Chesterton once wrote that the madman has not lost his reason; rather, he has lost everything *but* his reason. He has lost his sense of wonder, meaning, and humanity. We see this in the *scientism* of our day, which posits that the scientific method holds the answers to all meaningful human questions (though it happens to have nothing to say about what makes life meaningful).[137] Reason, then, and the scientific instruments and methods it employs, cannot by themselves supply our ultimate goals and ends, but they can be exceedingly useful means to reach the kind of truths that are within their powers. Let's look at some of the fundamental characteristics of logic, reason's most fundamental instrument.

Logic is the science of reasoning, the structure, principles, and methods of producing valid arguments that, if our starting premises are true, will make clear the further truths they imply. Along with such fundamentals as *metaphysics* (the study of being) and *ethics* (the study of virtue and morals), *logic* is another

---

[137] See "Scientism" in chapter 12.

essential branch and the indispensable tool of philosophy. Aristotle was its most profound pioneer and expositor, known as "the Father of Logic" by some and as "the Philosopher" by St. Thomas, who embraced and employed Aristotle's logical principles of reasoning in everything he wrote about. Indeed, in regard to matters of faith that may elude our unaided powers of reason, St. Thomas would write with exuberance:

> For when a man's will is ready to believe, he loves the truth he believes; he thinks out and takes to heart whatever reasons he can find in support thereof; and in this way human reason does not exclude the merit of faith but is a sign of greater merit.[138]

Thomas also wrote that humans are the only creatures we know of who acquire truths through the sequential steps of logical reasoning. As we saw in chapter 8, animals, lacking rational, intellectual souls, cannot understand and reason like man. Angels, on the contrary, are spirits without bodies. Their thought does not depend on information starting with any bodily senses and progressing in stages to the intellect but is characterized by the instantaneous knowledge of intuition.

Although logical reasoning is a step-by-step process, it is founded on a very few fundamental, *self-evident* principles we can grasp through our human powers of understanding, such as *the law or principle of noncontradiction*, which holds that "a thing cannot be and not be at the same time in the same respect." In other words, nothing can be both true and false or be what it is and what it is not. This is self-evident because we simply cannot think otherwise. If one were to argue, "But a thing can be both

---

[138] *Summa Theologica*, I-II, Q. 1, art. 10.

true and false at the same time!" one would be arguing that *that statement itself is true* and *not* false! The law of noncontradiction is founded on and stated positively as *the law or principle of identity*: "A is A," a thing is what it is, and not also what it is not in the same sense at the same time. Another is the *law of the excluded middle*, which holds that if a proposition is true, its negation must be false. There is no middle ground between truth and falsity. With foundations such as these, we can monitor our logical-reasoning processes to make sure these principles have not been violated, in which case our reasoning would be in error.

Indeed, Thomas explains that God, as Truth itself and the source and font of all truths, does not violate these principles. God would not and could not, for example, exert His power to make it so that something that happened in the past did not happen, for to do so would mean that something that truly *did* happen *did not*, that what was true is now false.

### Onward Now into the Deep

You'll recall from our introduction Thomas's advice to Brother John: when seeking truth, to "enter by the narrow streams, and not go straight to the sea; for difficult things should be reached by the way of easy things." Perhaps you have noticed that this book is structured according to Thomas's advice. We began with simple, commonsense maxims, and developed them in short chapters. As Father White observed in his commentary on Thomas's letter: "Only in the last paragraph of his letter does St. Thomas deal with methods of study in the strict sense, with purely intellectual procedures."[139] The paragraph to which he refers starts with the maxim: "Do not place value on who says what, but rather,

---

[139] Aquinas and White, *How to Study*, 26.

commit to your memory what true things are said." And yes, you are correct, that was the material of chapter 7. From that point on, as we delved into such things as the nature and perfection of intellectual powers, such as strategic memory and conceptual understanding, our streams got wider, our chapters got longer, and we had to put on our thinking caps.

Well, part 2 is for you stalwart readers who have made it this far downstream and are willing now to jump into some deep intellectual seas, further building your powers of memory while using your powers of reason to grapple with misuses of reason and distortions of faith, with logical fallacies, distorted ideologies, heresies, and half-truths that wreak so much havoc in our world. So then, I invite you to join me as I navigate our ship of thought and study into some deep, sometimes turbulent seas. With St. Thomas at our ship's helm, we will certainly reach the shores of newfound knowledge.

*Chapter 11*

# Reason Gone Wrong

## *A Guide to the Logical Fallacies That Lead Reason Astray*

*Again, if we are to avoid the errors which are the source of and fountain-head of all the miseries of our time, the teaching of Aquinas must be adhered to more religiously than ever.*

—Pope Pius XI, *Studiorem Ducem*

*To reason is to advance from one thing understood to another, so as to know intelligible truth. . . . Reasoning, therefore, is compared to understanding, as movement is to rest, or acquisition to possession.*

—St. Thomas Aquinas, *Summa Theologica*, I, Q. 79, art. 8

### *It's Hard to Reason Carefully about Things You Cannot Remember*

Of course you remember that "repetition is the mother of memory." Further, you might recall that I claimed our memory methods will allow you to come to know whatever you choose to remember "forward and backward." So then, it's time to see if you are still able to recall the themes of the ten precepts of our chapters that we first memorized in chapter 7 in our memory house's foyer. Do you still have them all? If not, rehearse some more, including rehearsing them *backward*. Can you work your way back through the mentalist failing in his trick in the drawer of the cushioned bench (location 10) to remind us of the precept of not seeking things too high for us; the overfull cupboard on a base with no ledge sitting on the cushion (9) to remind us of the admonition to fill up our cupboards of knowledge to the brim; the book standing under the power generator in a mirror (8) to remind us of our powers of reading, and of understanding; the tooth admired by Mnemosyne in the chandelier (7) to help us remember to commit cherished truths to our memory; Christ surrounded by saints in the center of the foyer (6) to remind us to imitate Him and those who follow Him; that entangling globe at the gun rack (5) to remind us to avoid worldly entanglements; the portrait on the wall (4) with the friendly and not-so-friendly men to remind us of the benefits and perils of friendliness to study; Thomas within the cell and the wine cellar as we peer out through the glass panel (3), reminding us to love to be in our study cells if we would be admitted to the wine cellar (or chambers of the king, if you prefer); the hands on the doormat (2) folded in prayer, emitting sparks to remind us of the power of pure prayer; and finally, Teddy Roosevelt at the front door (1) speaking slowly and carrying that big stick with a heart and a brain painted on it to remind us to "speak slowly and carry a big heart and mind"?

Got them all? Good! If not, please refer another time or two to the summary table in chapter 7 or in the Master Mnemonic Table in the appendix.

We have so much more to remember in the pages ahead, but since we will memorize concepts expressed in just one word or a brief phrase, I believe you will find them much easier to recall than the ten precepts, especially as your powers of memory continue to grow through these guided exercises. There is far too much to learn to cram into our memory foyer. Therefore, I invite you right now to follow me (or better yet, St. Thomas Aquinas) out of the foyer and into our adjoining mnemonic living room.

Ah, but first one piece of advice. Our memories operate best when they are fed digestible chunks of reasonable size. Therefore, I will dispense this mnemonic and intellectual feast in small servings of only five items at a time. Please feel free to learn five at a time, and then get up from the table, relax a bit, walk the dog, see to your other responsibilities, and come back another time to add the next five. Rome, after all, wasn't built in a day. On the other hand, if you are a stalwart soul with a ravenous appetite for knowledge, and you have the time and energy to spare, I invite you to see if you can consume, digest, and remember all twenty fallacies contained in this chapter without getting mental indigestion. In any event, this chapter's dinner will now be served in the living room, the dining room, and even in the family room!

## Logical Fallacies 1–5 (Locations 11–15)[140]

Now, the first odd thing that strikes you as you walk into this room is that Thomas himself greets you *in Latin*. Judging by the look on your face, which indicates that Latin may be all Greek

---

[140] They are numbered 11–15 in our memory tour since they continue within the memory house after the first ten locations we filled with the book's ten main themes in our exercise in chapter 7.

(unfamiliar) to you, he continues in perfect, modern-day English. I'll soon explain the reason for this.

For now, let's proceed into the center of the living room (location 11), where you find the first of seven quite *argumentative* people. The first one is the scariest because he is wielding in one hand what you first thought was a *vacuum* cleaner, but which, upon closer inspection, you see is really a big *club*. Next, gazing through the large picture window (12) into the backyard, you see an archaeologist arguing with an ancient-looking skeleton he has dug up there. "This skeleton," he yells to you, "is an early *Homo sapiens*." Going back into the living room and over to a sofa (13), you behold a scene just as odd, if not more so, for there sits a man who has just finished arguing with a human-size ant on the cushion next to him. Apparently, he has had enough, for his arms are folded and he has turned his back now, *ignoring the ant*. In front of the sofa is a large coffee table (14), on which sits an old *miser* wrapping a *cord* around a bag of money. Across from the coffee table is a wide-screen TV (15), and who should be on it but two of the nation's most *popular actors* arguing with each other.

So then, have you locked in your memory the man with a *club* that looked like a *vacuum* in the center of the living room (11), the archaeologist arguing with a *Homo sapiens* skeleton seen through the picture window (12), the man *ignoring an ant* on the sofa (13), the *miser* with his *corded* bag of money on the coffee table (14), and the *popular* actors arguing on TV (15)? I imagine that you have, but if not, please just rehearse them another time or two, and then I will show you *what else* you've just remembered, too!

All right then, it is time to reveal the serious abstract concepts those whimsical images help call to mind. We imagined

Living Room

an argumentative man with what looked like a *vacuum* but was really a *club* to help us remember the logical fallacy known in Latin as the *argumentum ad baculum*, meaning "the argument to the cudgel" or "the appeal to the stick," a false form of argument that really consists of a threat. The archaeologist and the *Homo sapiens* skeleton will call to mind the fallacy of the *argumentum ad hominem* (argument to the man), which attacks the arguer instead of the argument. The man *ignoring* the *ant* represents, of course, the *argumentum ad ignorantiam* (argument from ignorance); the *miser* and his *cord* represent the *argumentum ad misericordium* (the appeal to misery or pity); and the *popular* actors are playing the part for us of the *argumentum ad populum* (argument to the people).

These simple mnemonic images are based on homonyms and puns that remind us of the sound of the *names* of these logical fallacies. Some, like the stick-wielding man for the *argumentum ad baculum*, also lock in clues to their *meanings*. Fuller descriptions of their meanings will follow in just a page or two, once we've made sure we've memorized all their names. First, let's lay out all of this room's fallacies clearly for all to see—and remember:

| Location | Image | Fallacy |
|---|---|---|
| 11. Center of living room | Man with vacuum, no—stick | *Argumentum ad baculum* |
| 12. Picture window | Archaeologist and *Homo sapiens* | *Argumentum ad hominem* |
| 13. Sofa | Man ignores ant | *Argumentum ad ignorantiam* |

| Location | Image | Fallacy |
|----------|-------|---------|
| 14. Coffee table | Miser with cord and money bag | *Argumentum ad misericordium* |
| 15. Big-screen TV | Popular actors argue | *Argumentum ad populum* |

Oh, and lest I forget, Thomas began the tour of our living room speaking Latin because our first seven fallacies are presented with their Latin forms to show how long they have been known to logicians and because they are often still referred to by their Latin names. We'll remember the last two with Latin names as we head out of the living room in our next chapter's memory tour.

Now, let's dig in a little deeper, for if you would think like Aquinas, you would do well to learn every one of them, so as to be able to identify them and call them out whenever you might find them lurking about, trying to lure you or others from the truth.

**11. Argumentum ad baculum.** *Baculum* is Latin for "stick" or "cudgel," so this fallacy is also known in English as the "argument to the cudgel" or "appeal to the stick." It is the substitution of a threat of force for a valid logical argument for those who believe that "might makes right." It essentially says, "Agree with me—or else!" St. Thomas dealt with this tactic in his *Summa Contra Gentiles*, when he warned against religious beliefs that had spread not through the persuasive evidence of supernatural signs, but through force and armed violence.[141] Unfortunately,

---

[141] *Summa Contra Gentiles*, trans. Anton C. Pegis (Notre Dame, IN: University of Notre Dame Press, 1975), bk. I, chap. 6, art. 4.

we see that this form of "argument" has reared its violent, ugly head again in some modern-day Islamic radical extremists, and at the world's great peril. Still, no one people, region of the world, religion, or belief system has a complete monopoly on the *argument ad baculum*. We can see it, for another example, in some modern secular opponents of the freedom of speech in the United States in recent years, as some speakers invited to American college campuses have been prevented from voicing their arguments by crowds of people intolerant of contrary views, carrying and using not figurative, but literal sticks.

**12. *Argumentum ad hominem*.** Arguments "against the man" instead of his reasoning really boil down to insults rather than logical refutations. Perhaps the most common version of the *ad hominem* is called "poisoning the well." Here, something negative is stated about a person to discredit whatever arguments he might make, thereby bypassing the arguments themselves. I tried to illustrate this tactic with two that have been slung at me on a popular bookseller's website. In one attack, a commentator on one of my reviews of another author's book on evolution and language said that he saw that I believed in God and was therefore unqualified to comment on scientific topics (as would be countless Catholic scientists, from devout layman Louis Pasteur, the "Father of Microbiology," to the priests Father Gregor Mendel, the "Father of Genetics," and Father George Lemaître, originator of the big bang theory in cosmology). In another, a man attacked me for a book I wrote with arguments countering atheism — *before the book had been released*. I thanked him and noted that I looked forward to further reviews from people who had a chance to read it! I now see that both examples are no longer on the site, removed either by their authors or the website administrators. Unfortunately, in our time, we see these kinds of attacks used increasingly in political discourse — labeling, for example, religious believers or holders of particular political positions as being "against science" without any specific analysis of their arguments on particular issues. Such tactics have no place in the repertoire of those who think like Aquinas.

**13. *Argumentum ad ignorantiam.*** A person using this fallacious argument appeals to our ignorance or lack of knowledge by claiming that if we cannot prove that his statement is false, then it must be true. A favorite aphorism of my mentor in neuropsychology was "absence of evidence is not evidence of absence." Just because we do not yet have evidence of some phenomenon or condition, it does not mean it could not be present. This was frequently seen when patients whose family members suspected they had dementia were found to have normal cursory mental status by their physician or neurologist, but were soon after found, upon more thorough neuropsychological testing, to be in the early stages of dementia. This fallacy can also entail a misuse of the "burden of proof" in logical argumentation. If an atheist proclaims that God does not exist, then the burden of proof is on him to make his case. If a theist proclaims that God does exist, then the burden of proof is on him to make his case — as St. Thomas Aquinas did so well, appealing not to ignorance but to the highest capacities of the human intellect!

**14. *Argumentum ad misericordium.*** The appeal to misery or pity perverts the positive human capacity for empathy to circumvent the use of reason. If you tell your professor you need a certain grade to keep a scholarship or perhaps get into a particular graduate school, hoping to bypass his normal grading scale, you have employed this fallacy. (Having been an adjunct professor, I can attest that this fallacy is still alive and well!) It may be applied to even more serious and far-reaching issues, too. For example, an advocate of abortion might attack a person who opposes it as lacking in empathy for the welfare of the mother, sidestepping the issues of the welfare and very life of the child, not to mention the potential negative lingering effects on the mother's physical, mental, and moral well-being, the negative effects on the father, and on the nation that promotes the death of the future generations of its own citizens.

**15. *Argumentum ad populum.*** This argument "to the people" is an "appeal to the masses," also referred to as "the bandwagon fallacy." It asserts that some idea, product, or practice must be true or good if the majority or a vast number of people in a population believe it is true, use the product, or practice the activity. It appeals to a desire to fit in and be accepted by others, and teens may be especially vulnerable to such false arguments from their friends. "Why not do X, because everybody's doing it?" It is the kind of fallacy that my own mother used to warn my siblings and me about: "If all of your friends jumped off a cliff, would you jump off too?" In a sense, embracing this fallacy is an abdication of the use of our own reason, functioning at the sensitive level of a parrot or a sheep rather than as a rational human being made in God's image.

## *Logical Fallacies 6–10 (Locations 16–20)*

Now, let's move right along in our living room and meet the next five logical fallacies lurking there. Across the living room and under the chimney, you see now a fireplace (16) and standing over a pot inside is an argumentative man disputing with a fish that is starting to boil. You can tell by its ferocious teeth that it is a huge *barracuda*. Having had about enough of the odd and argumentative crew of the living room, you decide to make your exit. Arriving at the living-room doorway (17) you see one last strange and disconcerting scene, for there stands a *dictator*, yelling at a *simpleton* who is wearing one of those old-fashioned pointed dunce caps.

You cross the threshold and arrive at our dining-room doorway (18) which is partially blocked by the largest pair of dice you've ever seen, but you conclude that they are *false dice* when you see that the face of each one shows an overfull seven dots. Next, you spy the table. At its head (19) a giant pair of denim *jeans falls* from the chair, and you *see* it. Finally (for this chapter anyway), on the table's center (20) a man in military uniform loaded with medals and with shoulder epaulets loaded with stars, quickly paces around. You surmise that he seems to be a rather *hasty general.*

So then, do you remember the man and *barracuda* bickering at the fireplace, the *dictator* yelling at the *simpleton* at the living-room doorway, the *false dice* at the dining-room doorway, the *jeans falling* off the chair at the head of the table, and the *hasty general* pacing around the table's center? You most likely will if you simply rehearse them another time or two (and perhaps once in backward order, to lock them in).

As for what we have remembered, the *barracuda* represents the *argumentum ad verecundiam* (argument to authority). If, after examining its explanation in chapter 12, the image barracuda and name *verecundiam* do not automatically call to mind the fact that this is the argument from authority, please feel free to embellish your image using the "keyword method" to lock in its meaning. Mnemonic keywords trigger not only a word's sound, but its meaning as well. So, for example, you could imagine that this barracuda is wearing glasses and reading a book, because he is an *authority* on fish, or you could imagine him writing a book,

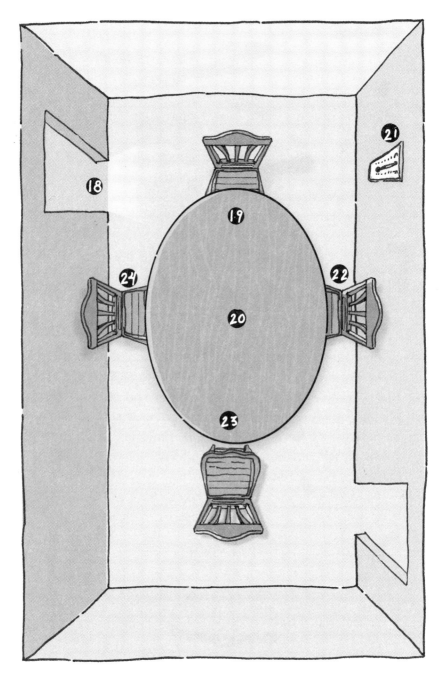

Dining Room

so the idea that he is an *author* will remind you of authority. You could even imagine him reading Aristotle or wearing a sweater with the name Aristotle on it, the ancient Greek being a favorite *authority* for many a scientist, philosopher, and theologian for centuries.

In what I hope was a wise use of metamemory (knowledge about how memory operates), I have not made all of our images explicit keywords that also lock in meaning, so as not to overwhelm your memory by making things unnecessarily complicated. Feel free to embellish your images to depict more of the meanings, if and when you find it necessary.

Now, where were we? Yes, the *dictator* and *simpleton* represent the *dicto simpliciter* that oversimplifies things. *The false dice* stand for the ever-popular fallacy of the *false dichotomy*, the *jeans falling* that you *see* serve to remind us of the *genetic fallacy* that circumvents addressing an argument by merely attacking its source or origin. Finally, the hasty general stands (well, paces) most fittingly, for *hasty generalization*. We'll dig into what they all mean next.

| Location | Image | Fallacy |
| --- | --- | --- |
| 16. Living-room fireplace | Man argues with barracuda | *Argumentum ad verecundiam* |
| 17. Living-room doorway | Dictator and simpleton | *Dicto simpliciter* |
| 18. Dining-room doorway | False dice | *False dichotomy* |

| Location | Image | Fallacy |
|---|---|---|
| 19. Head of table | Jeans fall, and you see | Genetic fallacy |
| 20. Center of table | Pacing military general | Hasty generalization |

**16. *Argumentum ad verecundiam*.** The Latin word *verecundia* denotes modesty and knowing one's place, but the fallacious argument *ad verecundiam* bespeaks an inappropriate and misplaced modesty that grants an authority more credit than it is due. It is probably known more widely as the "appeal to authority." Medieval thinkers are commonly caricatured as people who inappropriately appealed to authority to settle scientific matters, specifically the authority of Aristotle, in lieu of actually investigating them. Thomas does cite Aristotle many hundreds of times in his *Summa Theologica*, and in almost every "On the contrary" section of each article, he cites some kind of authority. What the modern "authorities" often leave out is that Aristotle himself was a great pioneer in scientific observation, being a father of biology, as well as logic. Further, the greatest medieval thinkers studied Aristotle both to embrace his truths *and to refute his errors.* Indeed, Thomas's teacher St. Albert the Great wrote an entire treatise on Aristotle's errors. Thomas himself wrote that "the argument based on human authority is the weakest." He cites authorities as starting points to his positions but always continues his "I answer that" sections with his own analyses.

Also, the partial quotation from Thomas provided above, writing as a Catholic, ended with the statement: "Yet the argument from authority based on divine revelation is the strongest," since God's own authority is indeed impeccable![142]

And, of course, how can we forget precept 7: "Do not place value on who says what, but rather, commit to memory what true things are said."

**17. *Dicto simpliciter.*** This fallacy involves stating a case too simply, ignoring exceptions to general rules of thumb. An example borrowing from our previous discussion of exercise in chapter 10 would be to declare that since barbell squats stimulate a greater hormonal response than any other exercise, everybody should squat. This would ignore the fact that, due to a variety of possible reasons, including significant damage to one's knees, back, or hips, or a severe heart or neurological condition, although squats are good in general, they could cause more harm than good for some people with special conditions. There is a sense in which this fallacy is contrary to the virtue of *gnome*, which Thomas writes about as an aid to the virtue of prudence. *Gnome* takes not only general rules, but special conditions into consideration before rendering judgments.

**18. False dichotomy.** This fallacy of "either-or" or "black and white" thinking presents the false dilemma of only two alternative answers or courses of action when there may be many more between the two extremes, or at times, when neither alternative is correct. A common false dichotomy present in self-proclaimed

---

[142] In a most fitting, and perhaps rather humorous manner, in the "On the contrary" article in which Thomas provides logical arguments for God's existence, the first authority he quotes is, in effect, God Himself: "It is said in the person of God: I am Who Am (Exod. 3:14)." From this unusual and ultimate appeal to authority, Thomas then proceeds to his famous five proofs that depend not on faith, but on reason alone.

"new atheists" is to propose that atheists believe, in accord with the findings of sciences such as astrophysics and geology, that the universe is billions of years old, while Christians believe, in accord with the Bible, that the earth is only about six thousand years old. This false dichotomy ignores the fact that only a small minority of Christians hold to fundamentalist interpretations of the Bible that run counter to scientific findings. Indeed, even seventeen hundred years ago, St. Augustine, bishop of Hippo in Africa, wrote that the Bible is not a textbook of science and that it should not be interpreted in ways that are contrary to human reason. Another common false dilemma some atheistic writers present is to argue that atheists respect reason while people of faith reject it. They cite statements such as this one from Martin Luther: "Reason is the greatest enemy that faith has; it never comes to the aid of spiritual things, but more frequently than not struggles against the divine Word"[143] — while failing to note that Luther was not a man who thought like Aquinas, who, centuries before Luther, had written that "human reason does not exclude the merit of faith but is a sign of greater merit."[144]

**19. Genetic fallacy.** This is a common variant of the *ad hominem* fallacy, in which an idea is rejected because of its real or supposed source, such as the psychological state or upbringing of the person advancing the argument. I recall a person who assumed that my reversion to Catholicism in my early forties must have been in response to a crisis, thereby implying that my belief in God answered a psychological need for comfort and assurance, rather than being a response to the Holy Spirit's promptings and

---

[143] Richard Dawkins, *The God Delusion* (Boston: Houghton Mifflin, 2008), 221.

[144] *Summa Theologica*, II-II, Q. 2, art. 10.

St. Thomas Aquinas's arguments. I responded, to the contrary, that my reversion occurred during one of the most serene and successful periods of my life. After having read and absorbed the philosopher Seneca's statement that "the busy man is least busy with living," I had stopped part-time college teaching on the side and had the most leisure and time for calm reflection in all of my adult life. We might recall yet again that one of Thomas's bits of advice on study runs directly counter to this fallacy in precept 7: "Do not place value on who says what, but rather, commit to your memory what true things are said." He was far less interested in the source of opinions than he was in their truth or falsity, and we would do well to think more like him.

**20. Hasty generalization.** This fallacy entails a failure in inductive reasoning,[145] jumping to an erroneous general conclusion based on far too little evidence. An example sometimes found in the writing of atheists is the argument that intelligent people such as scientists do not believe in God. They provide some examples of prominent intelligent atheists or atheistic scientists, while completely ignoring vast numbers of exceedingly brilliant, accomplished scientists and other thinkers who do believe in God.

## *Repetitio est Mater Memoriae (Again)*

Do you still recall the first ten logical fallacies? If so, that's great, and if not, it's time to brush up and rehearse them again until they are stored away securely in the treasury of your memory.

---

[145] Inductive reasoning starts from particular facts to reach general conclusions, while deductive reasoning, epitomized in the syllogism, starts from general principles known to be true to reach a conclusion about particulars.

Now we will add five more logical fallacies to our memory banks. Here we go.

### Logical Fallacies 11–15 (Locations 21–25)

Still in our dining room, we move now to a big wall thermometer (location 21), on top of which you spy (as you might have expected—or perhaps not) very tiny, *hyperactive* people *bowling*. Moving next to the chair at the right of the table (22), you find your grade-school principal, but she is very tiny. Indeed, she is a surprisingly *petite principal*. At the foot of the table (23) is a rather complicated scene, for a woman is *posting* a *hoc*key puck in the mail, whereupon *air* goes out of the odd, inflatable puck, and the postman tells her she really ought to send a *proper hoc*key puck. (Got all that? Perhaps it is easier for hockey fans, or perhaps for postal employees. No need to worry, though. Sometimes the extra effort that goes into complicated images makes them all the more memorable!) Moving now to the chair on the left (24), you smell something fishy, for there, flopping about, is the biggest *red herring* you have ever seen. Well, having about had your fill of the dining room, you head next to the doorway into the adjoining family room (25) and come across an odd scene, for a *con*victed criminal is writing a *text* and a guard then blacks *out* a section within *quotation* marks. Got them now? I'll give you a minute. Good! Let's see what we've remembered.

The *hyper bowlers* (21) stand for the fallacy of *hyperbole*, and your *petite principal* (22) represents the *petitio principii*, aka, "begging the question." (You might embellish this one a bit by imagining her begging a student to ask a question.) The *post*ing of the *hoc*key puck when the *air* goes out and the woman being urged to send a *proper hoc*key puck (23) represents the fallacy of *post hoc,* *ergo propter hoc* (because of the phonetic similarities, of course, and not just because the fallacy's name happens to come after the image description in that sentence). The *red herring* (24) stands for, well, the fallacy known as *red herring*. Its Latin name is *ignoratio elenchi* (ignoring the argument), but I couldn't resist using the English name since it makes for such a nice image! Finally, we see the *quotation* blotted *out* of the *con's text* to remind us of the fallacy of *quotation out of context* (25). Let's review:

| Location | Image | Fallacy |
|---|---|---|
| 21. Wall thermometer | Hyper people bowling | Hyperbole |
| 22. Seat on right | Petite principal | *Petitio principii* |
| 23. Foot of table | Posting hockey pucks | *Post hoc, ergo propter hoc* |
| 24. Seat on left | Red herring | Red herring |
| 25. Doorway to family room | Quotation out of con's text | Quotation out of context |

**21. Hyperbole.** This fallacy exaggerates and distorts true facts. It is very commonly found today in popular news reporting of scientific studies. For an example familiar to me as a psychologist, a headline may declare that a particular deficient brain chemical has been found to *cause* a disorder such as depression or schizophrenia, or at least that people with depressed or schizophrenic minds *have* this particular chemical deficiency, because a statistically significant number of patients in a study were found to have the deficiency. The headlines ignore the fact that in virtually all such studies, some people with the disorders do *not* have the chemical imbalance and some people within the normal control group and without the disorder *do* have the chemical imbalance. While such findings may show great value, producing hope for many people, to state that the imbalance *causes* a disorder based on imperfect evidence ignores the fact that the imbalance is neither a *necessary* nor a *sufficient* cause, since a person might have the disorder without the imbalance or the imbalance without the disorder.

**22. *Petitio principii*.** Better known as "begging the question" or "circular reasoning," this fallacy *assumes* from the start what it supposedly *proves*. St. Thomas addresses a particularly interesting and profound example when he argues that the existence of God is *not* self-evident to human beings.[146] He counters an argument stating that God's existence is self-evident to us because it is naturally implanted in us, employing both the logic of Aristotle and the words of Scripture, noting that for things that are self-evident we cannot think otherwise (for example, the fact that a whole is greater than its parts or that a triangle has three sides), and yet people *do* think otherwise about God's existence, as Scripture itself makes clear: "The fool says in his heart, 'There is no God'" (Ps. 53:1.) Thomas explains that God's existence *would* be self-evident to us if we understood the nature of His essence, since His essence and existence are one (it is His very essence to exist), but God's essence is imperfectly known

---

[146] *Summa Theologica*, I, Q. 2, art. 1.

to man, and that knowledge is achieved through reasoned argument or through revelation. An awareness of God *is* implanted in our natures, *but in a very confused way*. It is one thing to know that someone approaches, and another thing to know that (for example) it is Peter. All people seek happiness, but not all realize that our complete happiness (beatitude) lies only in God.

**23. *Post hoc, ergo propter hoc.*** To put it into English: "after this, therefore, because of this." This fallacy assumes that because one thing occurred after another, it must be the result of the first thing. For a month, a young man takes a scoop of Miracle Muscle Grow in his milkshake every day before his workout, gains five pounds of muscle, and attributes it to that expensive, but powerful miraculous powder, not thinking that perhaps his weight-training workouts, along with normal, healthful foods could have yielded similar results. This fallacy bears relation to superstitions and also to the placebo effect, wherein a certain percentage of the population derives positive effects from supposed "medicines" that are really inactive sugar pills. This is why scientific researchers include control groups and try to control as many other potentially relevant variables as possible to try to make sure that when they are testing for effects of some drug or other intervention, it is truly the cause of the effects, and not merely something that happened to come before them. Those who would think like Aquinas should bear this fallacy in mind in matters related to the proper care of one's mind and body.

I'll note as well that, in the realm of scientific research, the avoidance of a variation of this fallacy is also expressed in the valid dictum "Correlation does not prove causation." Just because two things tend to *occur together* does not necessarily prove that one *causes* the other, because either one might be the cause of the other, or both might be caused by some other factor or set of factors. For an extreme example, consider that, in children, shoe size correlates fairly strongly with performance on tests of intelligence. As shoe size increases, children tend to score significantly higher on tests of all kinds of mental abilities, from short-term memory, to mathematical calculation ability, vocabulary, reasoning, problem-solving, and more. This does not necessarily imply that we should figure out new ways to make our kids' feet grow, because that finding reflects the fact that not only *foot* size, but *brain* size and interconnections,[147] practical experience, and learning also increase dramatically from infancy into adulthood. Test children of the same age or test adults, and the correlation between foot size and intelligence pretty much disappears. Correlational studies can provide useful information, especially when subjects cannot be assigned to experimental or control groups for practical or ethical reasons, but they must always be interpreted with utmost caution when attempting to ferret out possible causative factors.

**24. Red herring** (*Ignoratio elenchi*). The Latin term refers to the fact that this fallacy ignores the real *elenchi* (argument) by

---

[147] I should note as well that even *brain size* has only a modest correlation with intelligence as measured by intelligence tests of people in the same age groups. It is estimated by some at a correlation coefficient of around 0.4, with 0.0 indicating no relationship and 1.0 indicating perfect correlation. I would suppose that St. Thomas did indeed have a large brain in keeping with his large body size (exact height and weight are unknown). We do know that Albert Einstein was of average height (reported to be between five foot seven and five foot nine) and average brain size, which does go to show that much more important than how much brain tissue we might have is what we choose to do with it!

diverting attention to something irrelevant. If you've ever accused someone (or been accused) of clouding the issue, changing the subject, or saying something besides the point, they (or you) may have been laying down a trail of red herring![148]

**25. Quotation out of context.** In this fallacy, a statement is selectively presented in a misleading way by ignoring the setting or context in which it is used. An extreme example culled from our discussion of the fallacy of the *petitio principii* could be to quote Scripture to *deny* God's existence: "There is no God" (Ps. 53:1). What a great difference a few preceding words make: "The fool says in his heart ..." Those who would think like Aquinas should exercise great care not to take Thomas's words out of context inadvertently. Returning again to our previous example, we find: "Therefore, the existence of God is self-evident." This however, came from one of the *objections* he went on to refute. When citing from the *Summa*, we should exercise great care whether the passages are from the objections, or the "on the contrary," "I answer that," or replies-to-objections sections.

### *Logical Fallacies 16–20 (Locations 26–30)*

It's time again to revisit our mnemonic house. Are the gists of all the precepts still tucked away in the foyer, along with the first fifteen logical fallacies in the living room, dining room, and

---

[148] The English phrase for this tactic has been tracked as far back as the late seventeenth century to references to laying down a trail of strong-smelling smoked or kippered herring to train dogs or horses to follow a trail while hunting. When not acting as a logical fallacy, the technique is also used at times as a literary device, as in detective novels when the author lays out false clues to try to lead readers away from the true conclusion.

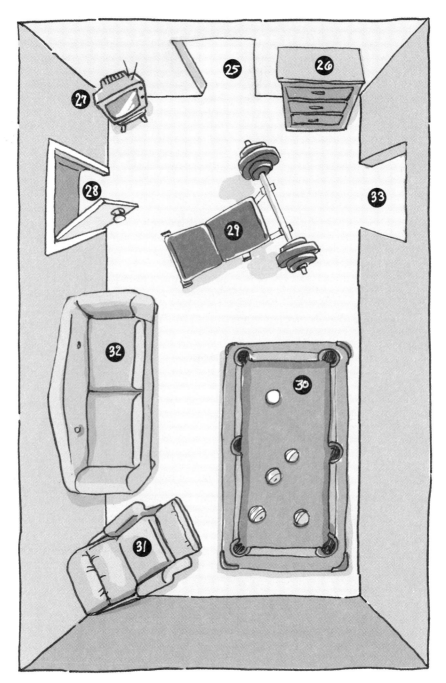

Family Room

doorway to the family room? Very good, if so! If not, be sure to find and put there any items that aren't waiting for you in their proper place. Now we will step into the family room and add to our mnemonic furnishings the last five logical fallacies of this chapter.

There is nothing odd about the tall, thin dresser (location 26) next to the door in the family room, except that it is *slanting* not unlike the famed Leaning Tower of Pisa. On the television set (27) on the other side of the door, a finely dressed "prosperity gospel" televangelist is hosting a TV *special* and *pleading* for donations. Right next door in the closet (28) is a *stereo*, which would not be unusual if this stereo did not have hands that are *typing* on a keyboard. Near the closet is a weightlifting bench (29), and who should be there pumping iron but the *scarecrow* from the *Wizard of Oz*. You're surprised by the weight he is lifting, having supposed that a *straw man* would be weaker. Finally, we arrive at our pool table (30), and you are highly honored, for the *secretary-general of the UN* has dropped by to tell you he *distributed* to all nations the *middle* section of the last *term paper* you completed while writing on that very pool table!

Okay, now it's time for the meanings. The *slanting* dresser (26) represents the fallacy of, well, *slanting*. The preacher on TV's *special pleading* (27) should remind us of *special pleading*. (Amazingly easy and straightforward so far, no? Well, it continues that way.) The *stereo typing* in the closet (28) should work well for *stereotyping*; the *straw man* on the bench (29) should work well for the *straw man* fallacy; and last, but not least, we come to the pool table (30), where the *UN* secretary-general who *distributed* the *middle* of your *term* paper will no doubt serve to remind you of the fallacy of the *undistributed middle term*! Let's chart all this out:

| Location | Image | Fallacy |
|---|---|---|
| 26. Dresser | Dresser is slanting | Slanting |
| 27. Television | Preacher's special pleading | Special pleading |
| 28. Closet | Stereo typing | Stereotyping |
| 29. Weight bench | Straw man lifting | Straw man |
| 30. Pool table | UN secretary-general distributes middle term paper | Undistributed middle term |

**26. Slanting.** This fallacy bears some relation to the *petitio principii*, or begging the question, because it attempts to skew the conclusion toward one's conclusion by the use of loaded words with strong positive or negative emotional connotations, in effect informing the hearer in advance what he is supposed to think and feel. We often see this in supposedly neutral and objective political reporting. A very simple example relating to religious belief is when some non-Catholics refer to Catholics as "papists" when criticizing Catholic dogma, implying from the use of that intentionally derogatory term that Catholics are followers of the pope, more so than of Jesus Christ. Of course, Catholics are not immune to slanting either, and we owe it to Christ, who is "the way, and the truth, and the life" (John 14:6) to keep our "paths straight" (Prov. 3:6) and not slanted as we seek to share the truth that leads to eternal life.

**27. Special pleading.** This fallacy involves setting standards for others that are not applied to oneself, by selectively omitting or overlooking information that would be detrimental to our argument. Lest I be accused of the same myself, let me make clear that to think like Aquinas is not to be infallible, even for St. Thomas himself, and neither would he have claimed it to be! His errors were amazingly few, though, considering the massive volume of his writings, and they rarely, if ever, involved philosophical issues. At times, he used scientific beliefs of his time as illustrations of certain principles that were later found to be untrue, though he did note his awareness that current scientific theories might later be proven false.

**28. Stereotyping.** This fallacy treats members of groups as if they were the same, assigning to each member characteristics attributed to the group that the individual may or may not possess. There are times when generalizations based on group membership can be valid rules of thumb—for example, that football players are very heavily built. Still, not every football player is very heavy. NFL football players average about 245 pounds, with the average tight end coming in at over a whopping 300 pounds, whereas other players, such as wide receivers and defensive backs, typically weigh much less. The kicker who holds the record for the longest field goal weighed less than 200. In its more egregious form, stereotyping implies that members of a particular sex, race, ethnicity, nationality, religion, or political organization all share certain negative characteristics. This is something those who would think like Aquinas should avoid. For example, while Thomas did not hesitate to criticize the theological errors of people who belonged to different religions, such as those of pagan, Jewish, and Muslim thinkers, he did not hesitate to welcome their ideas and quote their writings when he concluded that their insights were true.

**29. Straw man.** Don't want to contend with an opponent's powerful argument? Then attribute a weaker one to him! This fallacy of setting up a flimsy "straw man" instead of facing a real argument can sometimes take the form of a false dichotomy as well, like the one I noted that atheists sometimes use, framing atheism versus theism as a battle between the modern, educated man of science and the uneducated, backwoods Bible-thumper. The fundamentalist serves as a straw man much easier to knock down than the likes of an Augustine or an Aquinas. Thomas, incidentally, had no taste for battling straw men. He often states the arguments of the objections more cogently than those who held such objections and makes clear which authorities they drew upon, be they revered Church Fathers, or Scripture itself, before showing how their arguments fall short.

**30. Undistributed middle term.** We'll conclude with a formal logical fallacy that entails faulty deductive reasoning, because it is so commonly seen and sometimes with the most derogatory implications for its targets. Let me lay out an example in a syllogism:

White supremacists prefer candidate X.

You prefer candidate X.

Therefore, you are a white supremacist.

This is fallacious reasoning because the middle term is not "distributed." It is not a universal term that applies to all cases. The reasons you prefer candidate X may differ completely from those of white supremacists or may coincide on issues that have nothing to do with race. To think like Aquinas, we must be aware of how prevalent illogical thinking is in our culture in regard to many of life's most important matters, whether through unintentional ignorance or clear-sighted malice. We should strive to do our best to avoid such ignorance or malice, through our own ongoing efforts, ever in cooperation with God's grace.

# Chapter 12

# Premises of Sand

### *Foundational Intellectual Errors*
### *Destroying Our Modern Culture*

Everyone then who hears these words of mine and does
not do them will be like a foolish man who built his house
upon the sand; and the rain fell, and the floods came, and
the winds blew and beat against that house, and it fell;
and great was the fall of it. (Matt. 7:26–27)

So, if the ten precepts of Thomas's letter and our twenty
logical fallacies are secured in the recesses of your memory, it is
time to move along and memorize the first five of our "premises
of sand": the sandy "isms."

### *Erroneous Isms 1–5 (Locations 31–35)*

Still in the family room, next to the pool table is a recliner (location 31), and reclining there is *a* man who keeps shaking his
head, saying, "*Gee, I don't know about God.*" Next to him, on
the couch (32), is *a* second man who firmly scolds the first man,
saying "I have *a thesis* that proves there is no God!" You decide
this room is not for you and head to the door that leads out (33),

whereupon you are met by another *convict*, this one wearing a uniform with stripes, but oddly enough, also with *sequins*.

When you head out the door, you are most surprised to find that the adjoining "room" not only has cathedral ceilings but is a full-blown cathedral![149] At the back of this cathedral is a baptismal font (34), and dipping his fingers into it to bless himself is the largest *construction worker* you have ever seen. You can tell by his coveralls and the huge jackhammer slung over his shoulder. Indeed, you hope he doesn't accidentally sling it against the beautiful marble font. In the center of the church in front of the two main aisles of the nave (35) you are surprised to see a very *large person consuming* a massive meal. You assume he is just getting started, because many sacks from many fast food restaurants are piled up around him. We, however, have finished this chapter's tour, so let's see just what we've really seen.

A man on the recliner (31) who says, "Gee, I *don't know* about God" serves to remind us of *agnosticism*. The *a* stands for "without," and *gnosis* is Greek for "knowledge." We simply have him saying "Gee" to remind us of the silent "g" in the Greek word *gnosis*. A man on the couch (32) who claims to have *a thesis* proving there is no God, should remind us of *atheism*. The *con* with *sequins* at the doorway (33) is there to remind us of *consequentialism*, the belief that consequences are what make actions right or wrong. (Apparently the judge or jury thought that some act of our convict was wrong.) Upon entering the

---

[149] In his commentary on the oldest known text on this location memory technique, St. Albert the Great wrote that "some will place a church." Well, that's exactly what we're going to do now!

cathedral, our burly *construction* worker at the baptismal font
(34) serves to remind us of *constructivism*, which holds that man
not only builds buildings, but builds, in a sense, reality itself!
Finally, we come to an even burlier gent (35) *consuming* a massive meal to remind us of *consumerism*, the idea that material
things can bring us happiness.

| Location | Image | Premise of Sand |
| --- | --- | --- |
| 31. Recliner | A man says, "Gee, I don't know" | Agnosticism |
| 32. Couch | Man with a thesis that there is no God | Atheism |
| 33. Doorway out | Convict with sequins | Consequentialism |
| 34. Baptismal font | Construction worker | Constructivism |
| 35. Front center | Man consumes huge meal | Consumerism |

**31. Agnosticism.** Deriving from the Greek prefix *a-* for
"without" and *gnosis* for "knowledge," agnosticism claims that
we cannot know whether there is a God. More extreme forms
hold, in accord with other isms, such as relativism and skepticism, that we cannot know *anything* with certainty. Sometimes a
person describing himself as agnostic means only that *he* does not
know whether God exists (and may not have pursued the issue),
without implying that God's existence is inherently unknowable.

In his *Summa*,[150] St. Thomas succinctly demonstrated that we can validly reason *a posteriori*, from things already known and evident to our senses, to things unknown and unseen. As we saw above, in his five famous proofs, Thomas notes through observations that (1) things move or change, (2) there are effects and causes, (3) things exist for a time and then perish, (4) there are varying degrees of goodness or perfection in things, and (5) there is ordered or purposeful behavior in nature. Therefore, he argues, there must exist (1) a first or unmoved mover, (2) a first or uncaused cause, (3) a necessary being that cannot *not* exist, (4) a perfection of being from which lesser degrees of goodness flow, and (5) a first and final cause that provides for the order and governance of the entire universe.

Thomas holds that reason can indeed demonstrate God's existence and tell us important things about His attributes, such as His being all-powerful, all-knowing, unchanging, simple, and loving. These serve as preambles to deeper revealed truths of the Faith. Once again, in the words of St. Paul: "Ever since the creation of the world his invisible nature, namely, his eternal power and deity, has been clearly perceived in the things that have been made" (Rom. 1:20). This position is also Catholic dogma, as is made clear in the documents of the first Vatican Council (1869–1870): "If anyone says that the one true God, our Creator and Lord, cannot be known with certainty by the natural light of human reason and by means of the things that are made, let him be anathema."[151]

---

[150] *Summa Theologica*, I, Q. 2. art. 3.
[151] Pope Pius X, *On Modernism*, in *The Popes against Modern Errors*, ed. Anthony J. Mioni (Rockford, IL: TAN Books, 1999), 184.

**32. Atheism.** Atheism holds that it can be proven that there is no God. Its hold on modern culture is relatively small but growing. Recent research indicates that in the United States, in the brief period from 2007 to 2014, the percentage of self-reporting atheists nearly doubled from 1.6 to 3.1 percent of the adult population (while agnostics grew from 2.4 to 4.0 percent).[152]

Thomas's proofs for the existence of God were just briefly mentioned. I will simply note here that though it was quite rare in the 1970s, I myself was drawn to atheism by erroneous philosophical arguments. Although it took me twenty-five years to find they were faulty, my reversion to Christ and His Church took place in a matter of days after I first encountered the writings of St. Thomas Aquinas!

Some of the most powerful atheistic arguments I encountered posited that the idea of God was self-contradictory, superfluous, or unnecessary. The supposedly self-contradictory nature of the idea of God is still found in modern best sellers on atheism that argue that God could not be both all-powerful and all-knowing, because, for example, if He knows what He is going to do tomorrow, He is powerless to do anything different. The supposed superfluity of God is summarized in the statement "Existence exists" and in the question "Who made God?" Those who proclaim, "Existence exists" argue that the visible universe is the ultimate starting point and foundation and it makes no sense to ask where it came from. The question "Who made God?" implies that God is no ultimate answer to how things came to be because it leaves open the question of His own origin.

It was not until I was in my early forties that I found that Thomas had masterfully answered such arguments more than

---

[152] Lipka, "10 Facts about Atheists."

seven hundred years ago. As for the first, he notes that a contradiction arises only if we conceive of God as limited by time, as we are, having yesterdays, todays, and tomorrows rather than being fully actualized and existing in the eternal now. He provides this simple analogy: "He who goes along the road does not see all who come after him; whereas he who sees the whole road from a height, sees at once all travelling by the way."[153] As for the superfluity of God and the self-sufficiency of the universe, Thomas makes clear that since no natural thing can give itself its own existence or sustain it, there must be a being whose existence is uncaused, necessary, and the font of all things that do not exist necessarily. Astute and retentive readers might also note that to ask, "Who made God?" is an instance of the *petitio principii*, or begging the question, since it smuggles in the idea that God is something made that requires some previous cause, while Thomas explains thoroughly that reason shows us that God is the necessary, *uncaused* first cause, the source and font of all further causation.

**33. Consequentialism.** *Consequentialism* is an ethical position that judges the rightness or wrongness of our behaviors by their *consequences*. It can be contrasted with the *deontological* view of ethics that focuses instead on following moral *rules* and *duties*, deriving from the Greek *deont*, meaning "being necessary." Consequentialism is very prevalent today in various forms. *Utilitarianism* is a variant that holds that ethical behaviors are those that produce the greatest pleasure for the greatest number of people. One problem with such views is that they tend to bolster the notion that "the end justifies the means," implying that any behavior may be justifiable if it leads to some desirable

---

[153] *Summa Theologica*, I, Q. 14, art. 13.

end.[154] An infamous example is captured in a phrase from around the time of the bloody French Revolution: "You can't make an omelet without breaking eggs." A version is often attributed to Vladimir Lenin. Eventually, millions of human lives were sacrificed to the failed omelet of Communist Russia. Consequentialism may utterly disregard the kind of moral restrictions, duties, and rights that undergird deontological views. Further, it runs counter to prudence, which enables us to achieve virtuous ends only through virtuous means.

Still, to think like Aquinas about our moral actions is to transcend both consequentialism and deontology, for Aquinas teaches a *eudaimonism*,[155] or *virtue ethics*, that holds that morally right actions are those that lead to our ultimate happiness and fulfillment as human beings in a limited sense on earth and in the complete sense in heaven. Thomistic virtue ethics require that we follow God's laws as beings made in His image and likeness. Moral acts do follow the right rules and do lead to the best consequences in the long run, but they are grounded in the perfection of the human powers God has granted us through development of virtues that not only perfect our own powers but share them for the glory of God and the benefit of our neighbor. Pope Pius

---

[154] A sadly common example is found in the case for abortion, in which the end of providing the mother the choice of whether to carry a child for the remaining months of her pregnancy is seen to justify the destruction of the human life within her.

[155] From the Greek words *eu* for "good" and *daimon* for "spirit." Aristotle taught a natural eudaimonistic virtue ethics, and Thomas completed and perfected it with the Christian understanding of the nature of man and the supernatural perfection of man through the graces of God.

XI made this point quite clearly in this comment regarding St. Thomas:

> He brought the whole science of morals back to the theory of the virtues and gifts, and marvelously defined both the science and the theory in relation to the various conditions of men who desire to live the common everyday life and those who strive to attain Christian perfection and fullness of spirit, in the active no less than in the contemplative life.[156]

Thomistic virtue ethics transcends the prevalent but paltry consequentialist view that "no action is wrong if it causes no direct harm to others," with the view that actions are right when they help make us and our fellow man the best people we can be, in accordance with our natures as rational animals, made in God's image and likeness, and adopted, through Christ, as His sons and daughters.

**34. Constructivism.** There are different varieties of the theory of constructivism employed in education, psychology, and other social sciences. In its most innocuous form, constructivism holds that each person builds his own knowledge base through interactions with the world. In its extreme form, it holds that there are no objective, external facts or truths, because all knowledge is "socially constructed," built by particular groups of people to meet their particular needs. The constructivist's answer to Pilate's question "What is truth?" would be that it is whatever a particular group's consensus has decided it will be—for them, at that particular time. Constructivism is closely related to relativism and other isms we will consider here. As for a brief Thomistic

---

[156] Pius XI, encyclical *Studiorem Ducem* (June 29, 1923), no. 21.

assessment of the foundations of constructivism from Thomas himself:

> He who teaches does not cause truth, but the cognition of truth in the learner, for propositions which are taught are true before they are known, because *truth does not depend upon our knowledge but upon the existence of things.*[157]

**35. Consumerism.** Rather than a deep, false metaphysical premise about the nature of reality, this ism is as shallow as the practices it encourages. It abounds in the world of secular advertising and in the prosperity gospel or gospel of wealth in some Christian denominations. Its essence is captured, in the first case, by the phrase "the person who dies with the most toys wins" and, in the second case, by those who preach that God wants all His believers to be financially rich, and those who are not rich are somehow lacking in faith. Allied with the sin of avarice or greed, consumerism promotes the idea that we are what we have the capacity to buy.

From the Thomistic perspective, consumerism promotes an inordinate focus on material goods at the expense of higher, spiritual goods. The consumerist mentality keeps our focus at the sensory level common with the animals, rather than the realm of intellect and spirit. It encourages *curiositas*, excessive care about lesser things that impedes our studious focus on the things that matter the most, and *covetousness* or *avarice*, illicit desires, and actions to obtain them.

Thomas himself was certainly no consumerist, as a couple of incidents from his life ring out loud and clear. Surely, you'll recall

---

[157] *De Magistro*, third article, reply to objection 6, p. 78; italics added.

our story from chapter 4, when Thomas voiced his preference for a copy of St. John Chrysostom's *Homilies on the Gospel of St. Matthew* over all the riches of Paris. Another story tells of a rich man who conversed with St. Thomas through the streets of Paris and insisted that Thomas allow him to buy him a generous gift. St. Thomas requested that he buy him all the caged birds being sold on the street so that he could set them free!

Hopefully, you are now feeling quite at home with all the ten precepts and a full twenty logical fallacies tucked away in their proper places, not to mention the first five premises of sand. Now it is time to scoop up the next five sandy isms as we proceed further into our mnemonic cathedral.

### Erroneous Isms 6–10 (Locations 36–40)

Moving up to the altar of our mnemonic cathedral (36) you see an *emotional priest,* so moved, after the Consecration, by Christ's Real Presence in Body, Blood, Soul, and Divinity that tears flow down his cheeks. Next, you see the strangest site in front of the confessional (37): people holding Bibles appear to be bowing before a big dog named *Fido.* Up now to the front of the pews on the right (38), and who should be there walking back to his pew but your most (or least) favorite *history teacher.* Back now to the center back of the church (39), you see a cardsharp dealing the most unusual cards that crumble into sand as he calls out to you, *"I deal isms!"* At last we come to the space at the start of the center aisles (40) as a young child does his best to recite the national anthem, but stumbles a bit, saying "one nation, *individual.*"

And now for the even sillier ideas those silly images represent. The *emotional* priest crying in joy at the altar (36) simply serves to remind us of *emotivism,* the belief that all moral

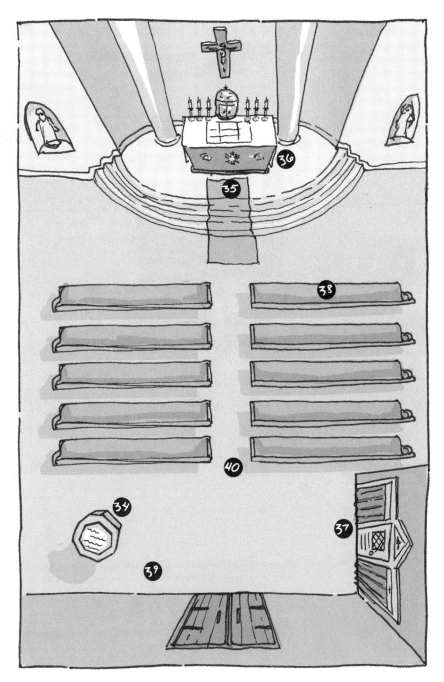

Cathedral

judgments are based on our feelings. Meanwhile, back at the confessional (37), the people with Bibles bowing before a dog named *Fido* are there to remind us of *fideism* (pronounced "fee day ism"), which holds that *all* truths about God and morals come from the revealed things of faith, thus discarding the role of our God-given reason. Your *history* teacher was walking past the front of the right bank of pews (38) to remind you of *historicism*, which overvalues the role of history in determining what we believe to be true. At the back of the church (39) was that cardsharp with crumbling cards who said, *"I deal isms!"* to remind us of, well, *idealism*, *which* understands our ideas as *that which* we think about, rather than that *through which* we think about things. Finally, back at the start of the center aisles (40) we saw the young lad saying, "one nation, *individual*" (instead of "indivisible") to remind us of the rampant *individualism* that breeds such selfishness in our day, by so focusing on our personal worth and dignity that we forget that all people are of worth and dignity, too.

| Location | Image | Premise of Sand |
|---|---|---|
| 36. Altar | Emotional priest crying | Emotivism |
| 37. Confessional | People with Bibles bow before Fido | Fideism |
| 38. Front pew right | Your favorite history teacher | Historicism |

| Location | Image | Premise of Sand |
|---|---|---|
| 39. Back of church | Cardsharp says, "I deal isms!" | Idealism |
| 40. Start of center aisle | Child: "one nation, individual" | Individualism |

36. **Emotivism.** René Descartes said famously, "I think, therefore I am." Emotivists effectively replace the word "think," with "feel." Emotivism, explicitly developed philosophically in the mid-twentieth century, holds that moral judgments are not based in thought or fact but are merely expressions of our emotions or feelings. It is common today for people to espouse emotivist views even if (or perhaps precisely because) they have never heard or thought about *emotivism.* It dovetails nicely with relativistic views (see "Relativism," below), which hold that the same moral actions may be right "for me" while wrong "for you," since people may feel differently about the same issues. It implies a great sense of tolerance—until what a person feels is not in accord with what you feel, or what you feel does not match what the perceived majority feels! Further, it removes the instruments of objective thought and reasoning that enable us to discover moral standards and find common ground between people who feel differently. In the Thomistic framework, emotivism lies stunted at the level of the sensitive soul. Humans, like the lower animals, have feelings, passions, and emotions, but they do not guide us to the true and the good without regulation by our intellectual powers. Natural virtues, including prudence, inform and guide our emotions to follow truths discerned from right reason, not from

how we happen to feel about some issue without having carefully thought the issue through in the light of objective reality.

**37. Fideism.** *Fides* being Latin for "faith," fideism is alive and well in modern times. In his encyclical *Fides et Ratio* (*Faith and Reason*), St. John Paul II warned against a fideism that "fails to recognize the importance of rational knowledge and philosophical discourse for the understanding of faith, indeed for the very possibility of belief in God" (no. 55).[158] We see this most commonly in "*Biblicism*," which makes the Bible "the sole criterion of truth."[159] Fideism is particularly dangerous in our time when it shuts off discourse between Christians and non-Christians. If Christians appeal only to the Bible about the existence of God or any moral issue, there is no common ground with people who reject the Bible's veracity. Human reason provides a common ground and a mutual starting point for every person who acknowledges the validity of rational argument. Thomas addressed this issue in many places, including in his *Summa Contra Gentiles*, which especially reaches out to nonbelievers by first appealing primarily to rational arguments. He writes, for example:

> Since there exists a twofold truth concerning the divine being, one which the inquiry of reason can reach, the other which surpasses the whole ability of the human reason, it is fitting that both of these truths be proposed to man divinely for belief.[160]

---

[158] *Fides et Ratio*, no. 55. See also the entry on *sola Scriptura* in chapter 13.

[159] Ibid.

[160] *Summa Contra Gentiles*, bk. 1, chap. 4. The two truths are those obtained through *reason* and those obtained from the *faith* produced by belief in God's direct revelation to man.

**38. Historicism.** St. John Paul II wrote of tendencies toward historicism prevalent in our time:

> The fundamental claim of historicism ... is that the truth of a philosophy is determined on the basis of its appropriateness to a certain period and a certain historical purpose. At least implicitly, therefore, the enduring validity of truth is denied. What was true in one period, historicists claim, may not be true in another. Thus, for them the history of thought becomes little more than an archeological resource useful for illustrating positions once held, but for the most part outmoded and meaningless now. On the contrary, it should not be forgotten that, even if a formulation is bound in some way by time and culture, the truth or the error which it expresses can invariably be identified and evaluated as such despite the distance of space and time.[161]

Not long after John Paul II wrote those words, I came across an article in the *Mensa Bulletin* of the American Mensa high-IQ society, in which the writings of Aristotle were referred to as "mere historical curiosities," implying that since they were written more than 2,300 years ago, they could obviously be of no real value to folks as enlightened as we are today.[162] In my printed response in the next issue, I commented that if Aristotle is a historical curiosity, I prayed that we might all become far more historically curious!

---

[161] John Paul II, *Fides et Ratio*, no. 87.
[162] C. S. Lewis deftly referred to this tendency to think of old ideas as inherently inferior to our own as "chronological snobbery."

*Historicism* misses the target of truth, both by overshooting the mark and *overvaluing* history (granting the time and circumstances in which truths are discerned more important than the truths themselves), and by *undervaluing* history (denying that perennial truths discovered long ago are just as true today as they were when first discovered or revealed).

Further, speaking of Aristotle (and Aquinas), just today I learned in John D. Mueller's *Redeeming Economics: Rediscovering the Missing Element* that in 1972 a major American university "abolished the requirement that Ph.D. candidates learn the history of economic theory before being granted a degree. The economics departments of most other major universities quickly followed suit."[163] Talk about *not* thinking like Aquinas! Even more interesting is Mueller's suggested remedy. He writes about a "missing element" that is found deep in the history of economics—within Scholastic economic theory—that "might be called AAA economics, because its basic formula is Aristotle + Augustine + Aquinas."[164]

**39. Idealism.** The *idealism* referred to here (more precisely called *epistemological idealism*[165]) holds that *sensation* gives rise to ideas, and when we think, we are conscious of our *ideas*. Although this may sound innocuous on its surface, in Thomistic philosopher Mortimer J. Adler's *Ten Philosophical Mistakes*, it is ranked the most profound and foundational mistake in modern thought! Those who think this way are clearly not thinking

---

[163] John D. Mueller, *Redeeming Economics: Rediscovering the Missing Element* (Wilmington, DE: ISI Books, 2010), 11.

[164] Ibid., 17.

[165] Epistemology is the study of knowledge and how we know what we know (from the Greek *episteme*, "knowledge").

like Aquinas! Here is the crux of the matter. Peek again at our diagram in chapter 8 labeled "The Birth of an Idea." Many modern philosophers since the days of John Locke cast doubt on the powers of the mind by supposing that *ideas* are the objects of our thinking or *that which we think about*, thus severing the direct connection between our ideas and the outside world. St. Thomas makes clear that *things themselves* are the objects of our thinking, and our ideas are primarily a means or *that by which we think about things*, although we *also* possess the self-reflective capacity to think about our thinking, when we are so inclined.

**40. Individualism.** Individualism is not a bad ism to hold if we take it in the general sense of a belief that acknowledges the worth and dignity of every single person, treating no person as merely the means to another person's or group's ends. Christ's words and actions proclaimed the value of every individual in the eyes of God, as He preached the salvation of every person who would take up his cross and follow Him, and He suffered torture and death to defeat sin and death so that we might attain everlasting joy in heaven.

Individualism is often corrupted into selfishness, however, placing one's own desires above the needs of others, denigrating or ignoring the value of loving relationships, while elevating one's own hedonistic pleasure. We see such individualism practiced and endorsed in many ways, at many levels. It occurs within families, for example, when an unhappy husband or wife desiring greater hedonistic pleasures forsakes his or her commitment and responsibilities to a spouse and children, legally divorcing the spouse, and to some extent, the children as well, as one's time and attention are drawn elsewhere. We see it, too, in the rising epidemic of loneliness in the modern world.

I found in my recent research into the problem of loneliness that psychiatrists (and spouses) Jacqueline Olds and Richard Schwartz expressed concern that America's primarily Protestant culture can overemphasize self-reliance and underemphasize the need for interpersonal connection. They cite sociologist Robert Bellah, who warned of "the near exclusive focus on the relationship between Jesus and the individual, where accepting Jesus Christ as one's personal Lord and Savior becomes almost the whole of piety."[166] Further, based on interviews he conducted, Bellah noted: "If I may trace the downward spiral of this particular Protestant distortion, let me say that it begins with the statement, 'If I'm all right with Jesus, then I don't need the church.'"[167] Those who think like Aquinas will always bear in mind that while every individual matters to God, who knows the number of hairs on everyone's heads (Matt. 10:30; Luke 12:7), we are made for relationships and are called to love God with all we are and our neighbor as ourselves, and not ourselves alone (Matt. 22:37; Mark 12:30; Luke 10:27; Deut. 6:5; 10:12; 13:3).

Let's do a quick review. Can you recall all forty of the virtues, fallacies, and faulty worldviews contained in our mnemonic foyer, living room, dining room, family room, and cathedral? If you need to double-check or study any of them further, please see the mnemonic master table in the appendix. If not, let's begin to study the contents of our very last room — quite fittingly, the study.

---

[166] Jacqueline Olds and Richard Schwartz, *The Lonely American: Drifting Apart in the Twenty-First Century* (Boston: Beacon Press, 2009), 37.

[167] Ibid. This is not to imply that all Protestants think like this — or that some Catholics do not, which would be a hasty generalization!

## *Erroneous Isms 11–15 (Locations 41–45)*

As you step through the study door (location 41) you are greeted by a saleslady bearing loads of colorful *material* across her shoulder, accompanied by a wispy figure you take for some kind of spirit. When you ask the saleslady what that figure is, she tells you it is not there. Next, you peer into a small bookshelf along the wall (42). A book entitled *Isms* captures your attention because of this memory tour, and when you reach out to grab it, a person with a strong Southern accent grabs it first, telling you, *"It's ma turn for Isms."* A tall bookcase (43) stands next to the short one, and you are dismayed when you see on the shelves medical specimens in glass bottles that appear to be *knees* and *heels*. Upon taking a closer look, you see that on the shelves of this bookcase there is really *nothing* at all. On top of the tall bookcase is a group of wrapped presents (44), and when you unwrap the largest one, you see an animal trainer inside with a small dog named Al (it's on a big name tag he wears). The trainer is using small mints for rewards, and when Al fails to sit on command, the trainer declares, *"No mint, Al!"* Finally, above the tall dresser is a picture on the wall (45); you feel as if it's déjà vu all over again when you see a painting of that person telling you *"It's ma turn* for *Isms"* again, except that the scene is painted in the setting of your local *post* office.

Now let's study just what the images in the study represent. The saleslady with material at the study door (41) stands for *materialism*, which, like her, denies the existence of a spiritual realm. The Southerner at the short bookcase (42) saying "It's *ma turn* for *Isms*," will remind us of *modernism*, the worldview that holds that our reason permits us to transcend the outdated truths of tradition. The tall bookcase (43) with the *knees*, *heels*, and nothing will remind us of *nihilism*, the view that holds that

Study

ultimately nothing matters. In the presents on top of the tall bookcase (44) we saw the trainer saying, *"No mint, Al!"* to remind us of *nominalism* (just remember: we're dropping the *t*). Let the dog in the image also remind us that nominalism holds that universal concepts are really just generalized names for particular things, thus denying the crucial distinction between the perceptual thought of animals and the conceptual thought of humans. Finally, in the picture (45) atop the tall bookcase, you saw the depiction in your *post* office of the Southerner saying "It's *ma turn* for *Isms*" again, to represent *postmodernism*, the view that we have now transcended even reason itself.

| Location | Image | Premise of Sand |
|----------|-------|-----------------|
| 41. Study door | Saleslady with material | Materialism |
| 42. Short bookcase | Southerner: "It's ma turn for Isms." | Modernism |
| 43. Tall bookcase | Knees, heels, nothing | Nihilism |
| 44. Presents on top of case | Trainer to dog: "No mints, Al!" | Nominalism |
| 45. Picture | Post office: "Ma turn" again | Postmodernism |

**41. Materialism.** Materialism can refer to the overvaluation of material goods, akin to that of *consumerism*, but here I refer to the more fundamental, metaphysical view that material things are all that exists, ruling out from the start the realm of the immaterial, the realm of the spirit, of the human intellect, the angels, and God. Materialists believe that nothing but matter matters. This view is predominant among self-proclaimed Darwinian "new atheists," who do not admit the existence of any kind of a spiritual realm. They think that if we cannot see it, hear it, taste it, touch it, or smell it, it does not exist—or that it is a mere byproduct, or even a delusion, with no significance of its own, such as the illusion of human free will or the delusion of God.

Many hold to this idea with obstinate passion. And yet neither we nor they themselves can see, hear, taste, touch, or smell their idea of materialism. How much does a consciousness raised by Darwin weigh, I wonder? What color is it? How loud might it be? If I say that it stinks or leaves a bad taste in my mouth, I'm merely being metaphorical. Atheists put science and reason on pedestals; how unfortunate it is that we can't take photographs of science and reason to hang on our walls to gather inspiration. Of course, science and reason themselves are "things" that exist not as matter but as the workings of the human intellect. Are they, then, any less real? You'll recall from chapter 8 that among the arguments for the human mind's immateriality is the fact that that human intellect is able to become, in a sense, all things, as it grasps conceptual forms abstracted from sensible matter. Further, none of the *thoughts* that you hold in your mind can be found through the operation of any kind of brain scan, biopsy, or chemical or electrical analysis, at the gross or microscopic levels.

**42. Modernism.** Modernism is a broad term encompassing several related erroneous philosophical and theological positions that became most prominent in the late nineteenth and early twentieth centuries but are still around. In his encyclical *Pascendi Dominici Gregis* (On Modernism) of September 8, 1907, Pope St. Pius X called it "the synthesis of all heresies." Some of its more prominent theological features are a rejection of the objective certainty of Tradition and established dogma in favor of the idea of the progress, evolution, and malleability of truths. With modernism came criticism of the divine authority of Scripture, dismissal of the miraculous, and the search for the secularized "historical Jesus." Its theories were bolstered by modern philosophy and the then-new theory of Darwinian evolution, and it placed greater emphasis on "personal experience" than on objective facts and revealed truths of the Faith. As for its remedy, Pius X wrote, "We admonish professors to bear well in mind that they cannot set aside St. Thomas, especially in metaphysical questions, without grave disadvantage."[168] Some decades later, Pope St. Pius XII would write on August 12, 1950, in *Humani Generis* (On Certain False Opinions Which Threaten to Undermine the Foundations of Catholic Doctrine) in section 31, on Thomistic Philosophy:

> As we know from the experience of centuries, the method of Aquinas is singularly pre-eminent both for teaching students and for bringing truth to light; his doctrine is in harmony with Divine Revelation and is most effective for safeguarding the foundation of the Faith and for reaping, safely, and usefully, the fruits of sound progress.[169]

Decades after that, St. John Paul II would concur: "The Church has been justified in consistently proposing St. Thomas as a master of thought and a model of the right way to do theology."[170]

---

[168] Cited in *The Popes against Modern Errors* (Rockford, IL: TAN Books, 1999), 230.

[169] Pope Pius XII, *Humani Generis*, in *The Popes against Modern Errors* (Rockford, IL: TAN Books, 1999), 358.

[170] John Paul II, *Fides et Ratio*, no. 43.

To think like Aquinas is to think like the Church, the rock that resists the passing winds of change that would reshape God in man's image.

**43. Nihilism.** Nihilism is from the Latin *nihil*, "nothing." Moral nihilism holds that there are no firm bases for any human morals or values. Writing about nihilism in the context of modern rejections of the power of reason, John Paul II wrote:

> As a result of the crisis of rationalism, what has appeared finally is *nihilism*. As a philosophy of nothingness, it has a certain attraction for people of our time. Its adherents claim that the search is an end in itself, without any hope or possibility of ever attaining the goal of truth. In the nihilist interpretation, life is no more than an occasion for sensations and experiences in which the ephemeral has pride of place. Nihilism is at the root of the widespread mentality which claims that a definitive commitment should no longer be made, because everything is fleeting and provisional.[171]

Note how nihilism reduces us to sensations and experiences of the sensitive soul, positing no real truths or worthwhile goals. There is a sense in which nihilism can be seen as the very antithesis of speculative wisdom and practical prudence. Wisdom and prudence focus on matters that matter the most, while nihilism holds that nothing really matters much. Like relativism, it holds that there are no objectively right or wrong behaviors. A deeply embraced nihilism bespeaks pessimism and despair for one's own life and denigrates the value and meaning of the lives of others. There is growing concern that the recent rise of horrendous

[171] Ibid., no. 46.

mass murders of innocent victims may be the fruit of the moral depravity of extreme nihilism.

**44. Nominalism.** *Nominalism* (from the Latin *nomen*, "name") has some kinship with epistemological idealism in that it denies any direct connection between our abstract or universal concepts and the outside world. It declares that only sensible individual things exist and that general universal terms, for example, "humanity" or "abstract entities," or geometric forms such as a triangle, are merely names or labels we use to describe particular things. Nominalism, therefore, denies the intellectual soul's crucial powers of abstraction and leaves us with perception but without valid conceptual thought.

Diametrically opposing nominalism is Plato's exaggerated *realism* of his theory of forms, which holds that perfect universals, such as humanity or triangularity exist in some higher realm beyond the reach of the senses. We see on earth merely dim and imperfect copies.

Moderating between both extremes is Aristotle's stance, aptly called *moderate realism*, which holds that universal concepts do accurately reflect essences of particular realities. We do form abstract concepts of the common essences of things, such as people as "rational animals" or triangles as "closed plane figures with three straight sides and three angles." Though the essences, such as humanity or triangularity, do not exist in and of themselves in some other realm, they can be accurately applied to identify essential attributes, and to differentiate particular, individual things. As we saw in chapter 8, to think like Aristotle, in this case, is to think like Aquinas.

**45. Postmodernism.** Postmodernism, in its extremes, is like modernism on steroids with 'roid rage against reason! Postmodernism took to the roads in France in the mid-twentieth century and is a synthesis and logical culmination of old and modern errors such as skepticism, constructivism, and relativism that denies the power of reason to grasp objective reality because there is no objective reality to grasp. According to this view, what have historically been called "truths" are not based on any kind of actual correspondence between reality and our thoughts about it but have been established to fit the needs of whatever groups happened to be in power at the time they were fashioned. Since postmodernists deny the validity of reason, you might surmise that it can be a little difficult to reason with them. Further, feeling free from the constraints of objective reality, at times their writings can get a little bizarre. My favorite exposé of postmodernist thought was truly a grand variation of an argument *ad absurdum*.[172]

In 1996, physicist Alan Sokal published an article entitled "Transgressing the Boundaries: Toward a Transformative Hermeneutics of Quantum Gravity" in the journal *Social Text*. Perhaps that title generated a "What on earth is the author even saying?" response in you. Well, it apparently did not to the editors of the avant-garde, "postmodernist" journal in which it was published.

You see, in 1998, the article's creator produced the book *Fashionable Nonsense: Postmodern Intellectuals' Abuse of Science*,[173] in which he and the book's coauthor, Jean Bricmont, revealed that Sokal's article was indeed a hoax, fabricated gobbledygook that made no sense whatever—and the journal's own editorial staff was *not* in on the joke! Sadly, such lack of clarity, meaning, and

---

[172] A valid technique of logical reasoning that demonstrates that if an argument is followed to its logical conclusion, it leads to absurd or contradictory results.

[173] Alan D. Sokal and J. Bricmont, *Fashionable Nonsense: Postmodern Intellectuals' Abuse of Science* (New York: Picador USA, 1998).

truth seems to make little difference in some postmodern academic circles. Sokal wrote the article as a protest against some contemporary postmodern humanist writers who played loosely with theories in math and science (not to mention with language), and whose writings, in effect, argued against objective truth, common sense, and reason.

### *Erroneous Isms 16–20 (Locations 46–50)*

We move now to the second of four sections of the study, and we stop first at the first of two swivel rockers (location 46). Upon the rocker sits a *mat* and upon the mat a *rag* with an embroidered letter *P*. (Got that?) There's a very odd tall lamp (47) next to the chair, for it has a vibrating belt attached to it, like those old electric purported *reducing machines*. On the other side of the lamp is a second swivel rocker (48), and it is apparently a really good one, since all of your *relatives* are trying to sit down in it at the same time! Now, between the two chairs is a cushioned footrest (49) and sitting on it is a *white-coated man* hunched over a *microscope*. You deduce that he is a *scientist*. Finally, behind the lamp and chairs is a large picture window (50), and as you peer at the front yard, you spy a group of four people *skipping* a rope, double Dutch,[174] and they call out to you, *"Why not skip this ism?"*

All right then. The *"P" rag* on the *mat* on the first rocker (46) stands for *pragmatism* (of course) which holds that the criterion for truth is simply whatever works. The tall lamp (47) is acting as an old *reducing* machine to call *reductionism* to mind, though

---

[174] Double Dutch is a game in which one or more persons jump between two ropes that are turning in opposite directions. If you are so inclined, try this sometime, but only with your doctor's permission!

reductionism, like materialism, does not hold that mind really matters.[175] Your *relatives* are crowding into the second rocker (48) to remind us of *relativism*, the idea that there are no absolute truths, ironically held by relativists as if it were an absolute truth! Sitting there on the footstool (49), that white-coated *scientist* hunched over a microscope will surely remind us of *scientism*, which acts as if all kinds of truths could be found through the methods and instruments of science. Finally, those rope skippers you see out the picture window (50) wanted you to "*Skip this ism,*" so you would not think too deeply about the way skeptics themselves never act as if they believed *skepticism* was true. Of course, if they were true skeptics, they could not be sure you were really there to hear them, that there really existed a rope to skip, or that they themselves existed!

| Location | Image | Premise of Sand |
|---|---|---|
| 46. First chair | "P" rag, mat | Pragmatism |
| 47. Tall lamp | Reducing machine | Reductionism |
| 48. Second chair | All your relatives | Relativism |
| 49. Footrest | Scientist hunched over microscope | Scientism |
| 50. Picture window | Skippers say, "Skip this ism!" | Skepticism |

---

[175] As it happens, neither the old vibrating reducing belt nor reductionism really works!

**46. Pragmatism.** Pragmatists hold that the proper function of human thinking is the solving of practical problems, which may well change over time, rather than accurately grasping facts of reality. Pragmatism holds that the true is that which works in practice; it disregards theoretical principles and foundational values. St. John Paul II warned of the growing prevalence of pragmatism at the end of the twentieth century after his discussion of scientism:

> No less dangerous is *pragmatism*, an attitude of mind which, in making its choices, precludes theoretical considerations or judgements based on ethical principles. The practical consequences of this mode of thinking are significant. In particular there is growing support for a concept of democracy which is not grounded upon any reference to unchanging values: whether or not a line of action is admissible is decided by the vote of a parliamentary majority. The consequences of this are clear: in practice, the great moral decisions of humanity are subordinated to decisions taken one after another by institutional agencies. Moreover, anthropology itself is severely compromised by a one-dimensional vision of the human being, a vision which excludes the great ethical dilemmas and the existential analyses of the meaning of suffering and sacrifice, of life and death.[176]

To those who think like Aquinas, any moral action that truly *works* operates in accordance with man's true and enduring nature and value as made in the image and likeness of God (Gen. 1:26).

---

[176] John Paul II, *Fides et Ratio*, no. 89.

**47. Reductionism.** Extreme reductionist views hold that complex phenomena can be explained most fully by the operations of their simplest, most fundamental parts. For example, the processes of biology can be reduced to those of chemistry, and chemical reactions to those of physics, while ignoring or downplaying the importance and interaction of processes at the various levels of complexity. This tendency may be seen in modern psychiatry if there is an overemphasis on mental disturbance as a result of chemical imbalances in the brain, while ignoring that a person's thoughts and physical activities can also impact physiological processes that regulate the stimulation of various hormones and chemicals throughout the body, including the brain. Think back on the last time something scared you for an example of how our perceptions of events in our lives can dramatically impact our body chemistry and physiological reactions.

For nearly the first half of the twentieth century, reductionist views held sway in the field of behavioral psychology, prompting the Russian psychologist Lev Vygotsky to argue that to study external stimuli and people's responsive reflexes without consideration of the workings of the human mind is like trying to understand the properties of water in relation to fire by only separately studying hydrogen, which burns, and oxygen, which sustains combustion.

As we saw in our look at *materialism*, among the most common and disastrous species of reductionism in our day is that which reduces the human mind to the brain, ignorant of the Aristotelian and Thomistic proofs of the mind's immateriality and the brain's role as its instrument. *Determinism* that denies the existence of free will is a common bedfellow of materialism and reductionism. In this view, free will is an illusion and our behaviors are all caused or determined by previous chains of events and experiences (including, one would then surmise, not only belief in free will, but belief in determinism as well).

**48. Relativism.** No, *relativism* is not about giving choice jobs to one's unqualified family members. (That's *nepotism*.) *Relativism* refers to a far more serious and pervasive premise that can leave all manner of destruction in its wake. Indeed, in our time, the man who would soon become Pope Benedict XVI warned: "We are building a dictatorship of relativism that does not recognize anything as definitive and whose ultimate goal consists solely of one's own ego and desires."[177]

Relativism replies to Pilate's question, saying that one thing might be "true for me" and another quite different thing "true for you" or for someone else. It most often takes the form of moral relativism and denies common moral truths, thereby seeking to remove limits on many behaviors commonly found harmful or unnatural throughout most of the history of humanity. Part of the reason is that it denies any such thing as a definite human nature. Ironically, however, this apparently tolerant stance that ostensibly allows everyone his own truths is marked by the greatest intolerance for those who believe there *is* absolute truth, there are statements that are true or false, and there are behaviors that are moral or immoral, regardless of who posits the arguments or engages in the behavior. From a Thomistic perspective, relativism rejects the nature of truth and the laws of logical reasoning, such as the principle of noncontradiction, and it also rejects the manner and methods of human understanding, from the fact that our senses provide us reliable information about the outside world, to

---

[177] Joseph Cardinal Ratzinger, Homily at the Vatican basilica, April 18, 2005, http://www.vatican.va/gpII/documents/homily-pro-eligendo-pontifice_20050418_en.html.

the fact that we can grasp abstract truths and communicate them meaningfully with others.

**49. Scientism.** If *fideism* is the Scylla that drives us off the course of truth in one direction, then *scientism* is the Charybdis that threatens to sink us when we veer off course in the other direction. The word *scientism* was not in use in Thomas's time. Per St. John Paul II, it is "the philosophical notion which refuses to admit the validity of forms of knowledge other than those of the positive sciences; and it relegates religious, theological, ethical, and aesthetic knowledge to the realm of mere fantasy."[178] Indeed, we have seen in just the last year or so a popular media scientist argue that not only *faith* but also the discipline of *philosophy* are irrelevant and contrary to science.[179] The dismissal of philosophy as well as religion is a real peril of scientism. Philosophy can examine data that a purely materialistic science must ignore or write off as a cumbersome byproduct of atoms and genes — namely, human interior experience, or what it means to be you or to be me. Further, philosophy can address questions of what we "should" do, as well as what we "can" do. Science can tell us, for example, how to make deadly weapons, while philosophy can address whether, and under what circumstances, it might or might not be right to use them. This is part of the reason why St. John Paul II warns against misunderstanding

---

[178] John Paul II, *Fides et Ratio*, no. 88.

[179] To his credit, this famous "science guy" later brushed up a bit on philosophy and acknowledged its usefulness. A simple Web browser search of "philosophy science guy" will lead you to the details. (By the way, I don't come out and name names in this section, so as to avoid any possible *ad hominem* attacks and to focus more on *arguments* than on *arguers* — who sometimes even change their minds!)

the limits of science, of a scientism that thinks we need only concern ourselves with material facts, and not with the ethical implications of those facts (for *ethics*, too, is a branch of philosophy):

> In the field of scientific research, a positivistic mentality took hold which not only abandoned the Christian vision of the world, but more especially rejected every appeal to a metaphysical or moral vision. It follows that certain scientists, lacking any ethical point of reference, are in danger of putting at the center of their concerns something other than the human person and the entirety of the person's life.[180]

When a person embraces scientism, he lets go of the highest parts of himself, of his neighbors, and of the God who created us all. In Thomas's terminology, we could say that the embracer of scientism is one who makes the intellectual virtue of science all there is to intellectual virtue, focusing on lower-order secondary causes and effects, while ignoring the fundamental principles on which they are based (the realm of *understanding*) and the final, highest, primary cause responsible for all of the facts of creation (the realm of *wisdom*, seeking knowledge of God), not to mention the realm of human moral actions, the realm guided by of the virtue of *prudence*.

**50. Skepticism**. Skepticism goes way back to the Greek philosopher Pyrrho (ca. 360–ca. 270 B.C.) and his followers. Pyrrho has many modern-day adherents, too, whether they realize it or not. Skepticism is the stance of doubt that holds that we cannot obtain certain knowledge about anything.

---

[180] John Paul II, *Fides et Ratio*, no. 46.

# How to Think Like Aquinas

A humorous ancient response to skepticism is found in the writings of the Stoic philosopher Epictetus (A.D. 55–135). In refuting the followers of Pyrrho of his day, Epictetus provides several delightful arguments *ad absurdum*. Here is one of the tersest from a live public lecture: "When I want to swallow something, I never take the morsel to *that* place instead of *this*.... And do you, who take away the evidence of the senses, do anything else?"[181] Truly, ancient skeptics acted in their daily lives as if they believed their senses did indeed supply them with accurate information.

As for one modern follower, some years ago, a skeptical co-worker, waxing philosophical, said to me, "You know, we can't be sure about anything," to which I simply responded, "Hmm, are you *sure* about that?" He chuckled and walked away without responding. To point out philosophical skepticism's contradictory, self-refuting nature is no guarantee its adherents will give it up, but those who would think like Aquinas should be well aware of the fact that skeptics cast doubt upon the workings not only of their own intellectual powers, but of their sensitive powers, too. In a way, the only thing a skeptic does not doubt is doubt itself.

Is it likely he's aware of this?

I doubt it.

---

[181] *Epictetus: Discourses, Books I-II, the Enchiridion*, trans. William Abbott Oldfather (Cambridge, MA: Harvard University Press, 2000), bk. 1.27, p. 487. Oldfather speculates that perhaps Epictetus gestured toward his mouth and then his eye, since he does mention the eye in a later, similar passage (bk. 2.20). Still, he suggests that the blunt and colorful Epictetus, perhaps inspired by the rather coarse Cynic Diogenes, may have pointed in this instance to a different part of his body!

*Chapter 13*

# Wrong Thinking about the Faith

## Two Thousand Years of Heresies and Half-Truths

> He [the heretic] chooses not what Christ really taught,
> but the suggestions of his own mind. Therefore, her-
> esy is a species of unbelief, belonging to those who pro-
> fess the Christian faith, but corrupt its dogmas.

—St. Thomas Aquinas, *Summa Theologica*, II-II, Q. 11, art. 1

> With his own hand he vanquished all errors of an-
> cient times; and still he supplies an armory of weap-
> ons which bring us certain victory in the conflict with
> falsehoods ever springing up in the course of years.

—Pope Leo XIII on St. Thomas Aquinas, *Aeterni Patris*

On now to the next section of the study as we move into special isms that deal not only with the nature of truth in general, of thought, or of moral behaviors directed by human reason, but also with the revealed truths of the Faith passed down from God's revelations and interpreted by the one, holy, Catholic, and apostolic Church that Christ built upon Peter, "the rock"

(Matt. 16:18). They are a sample of some of the most prominent *heresies*, popular beliefs throughout the centuries that distorted the Church's orthodox teachings about the Faith, including the nature of God, of creation, of man, of Jesus Christ, and of His Blessed Mother. They will be fleshed out, as usual, after our five-at-a-time mini memory tours. So now let's see where they are lurking in our memory house.

### Heresies and Half-Truths 1–5 (Locations 51–55)

In the corner of the study you find a globe (51), and, zooming in on Germany, you see a disturbing scene from the late 1930s, for there is a wildly gesticulating Adolf Hitler haranguing a crowd about the "Aryan master race." Next to the globe is yet another bookcase (52), and, odd as this may seem, you see atop it a little *bed* from which your friend or relative *Cathy* (whom you call "Cath") has just *arisen*. Across the room at the doorway out of the study (53) you find a heretic with a foreign accent struggling to stick a big letter G on the doorjamb. He says to himself, "G *no stick!*" Upon the wall opposite the picture window hang five diplomas (54). You may not believe this, but our heretic at first tries to arrange them neatly on the wall by some kind of category but decides to rip them all down instead, saying to himself: "*I cannot class them!*" Lastly, we come to a picture on the wall (55) that rests over the globe, and who should be pictured there but your friend *Jan's son!* (Your friend Jan has no son? Or you don't even have a friend named Jan? That's not a problem for our purposes. You need merely imagine them!)

The globe (51) with Hitler proclaiming *Aryanism* will remind us of the heresy of *Arianism*, which provided not only a distorted view of humanity but denied the divinity of Jesus Christ. From the bed atop the bookcase (52) we saw *Cath arisen* to remind us of the heresy of *Catharism*, held by people who thought they were pure and that the body was evil. The accented heretic in the doorway (53) said, "G *no stick!*" to remind us of *gnosticism* (though our *g* is silent). *Gnosis*, as we've seen, is Greek for "knowledge." While *a*gnostics hold that we can't know about God, gnostics hold that they have secret spiritual knowledge. The heretic who said, "*I cannot class them!*" and tore the diplomas (54) off the wall is there to remind us of the heresy of *iconoclasm*, which held that religious icons, be they pictures or sculptures, should be torn down from their walls. Finally, *Jan's son* in the picture (55) reminds us of *Jansenism*. We might imagine that Jan put that son's portrait on the wall because she believes he is one of God's chosen elect. Being a Jansenist, she believes that God has elected certain people to enjoy heaven and others to suffer hell, and what we do with our free will does not even enter into the picture, so to speak.

| Location | Image | Heresy |
|----------|-------|--------|
| 51. Globe | Hitler touts Aryanism | Arianism |
| 52. Bookcase | Cath arisen from bed | Catharism |
| 53. Doorway out | Heretic: "G no stick!" | Gnosticism |
| 54. Diplomas | Heretic: "I cannot class them!" | Iconoclasm |
| 55. Picture | Jan's son | Jansenism |

**51. Arianism.** Arianism is named after the Alexandrian priest Arius (A.D. 256–336), who consolidated and spread widely early heretical ideas that Jesus Christ could not have had both divine and human natures, holding that Jesus was not eternally one with God but was at some point created by Him, and then through Jesus creation was completed. In a sense, the heresy is an effect of elevating reason above faith because human reason is unable to grasp fully the mystery of Christ's two natures and that the eternal Son of God, could, at a point in time, become incarnate as man. It is because of the powerful influence of the Arian heresy that we proclaim at Mass each Sunday that Christ is "begotten, not made, consubstantial with the Father," echoing the pronouncement of the Council of Nicaea in 325 that Christ is *homoousios to Patri:* "of one substance with the Father."

Of his many writings on Christ's nature in the third part of the *Summa Theologica*, I'll highlight here one that refers both to Scripture and to St. Athanasius (296–373), bishop of Alexandria and Arian's greatest theological opponent.[182] Thomas writes: "On the contrary, it is written (John 1:14): 'The Word was made flesh'; and as Athanasius says (*Letter to Epictetus*), when he said, 'The Word was made flesh,' it is as if it were said that God was made man."[183]

A form of Arianism remaining in our day is *Unitarianism*, though St. Athanasius argued that Arianism reintroduced *polytheism*, since Christ was to be worshipped as a separate, lesser god.

---

[182] In his *Thirty-Ninth Festal Letter* to his flock around Easter in 367, Athanasius presented for the first time in history a list of the twenty-seven books that would come to be pronounced by the Catholic Church as the official canon of the New Testament for all of Christianity. (Let's keep that in mind when we come to our last heresy.)

[183] *Summa Theologica*, III, Q. 16, art. 6.

Perhaps the most prevalent derivative of Arianism in our time is to deny Christ's divinity and view Him merely as one among several great ethical teachers.

**52. Catharism.** Deriving its name from the Greek *katharoi*, "pure ones," this heresy began to flourish in the eleventh century in the Languedoc region in southern France, especially in the city of Albi; hence, it was also known as the *Albigensian heresy*. It was a mixture of Christian and non-Christian beliefs that included a variety of dualistic beliefs, most prominent among them being that there exists a god of goodness and a god of evil. The god of goodness created spiritual things and is the god of the New Testament, while the god of evil created the material world, including the human body. Among their stranger beliefs were the permissibility of fornication, since the body was not important, and the avoidance of marriage and reproduction so as to prevent spirits from becoming trapped inside bodies.

That such thinking is diametrically opposed to the thought of Thomas Aquinas is clear for many reasons, one of the most obvious being their denigration of the body, since Thomas's entire human anthropology and psychology are based on the nature of humans as God-crafted *hylomorphic* (matter-form), body-soul composites. Thomas, of course, was also a Dominican, a member of the religious Order of Preachers, founded by St. Dominic de Guzman (1170–1221). One of Dominic's earliest missions was the conversion of the Albigensians. In a famous incident early in his ministry, he stayed up all night talking to an Albigensian innkeeper and brought him back to Christ and the Catholic Church.

**53. Gnosticism.** Gnosticism, deriving from the Greek *gnosis* for "knowledge," is a very early heresy with Greek, Jewish, and other ancient Middle-Eastern philosophical and religious roots and branches. It held itself as a special form of knowledge that recognized the evil of matter and the goodness of spirit, as would Catharism centuries later. This, of course, runs directly counter to the goodness of creation repeatedly proclaimed in the book of Genesis (1:10, 12, 18, 21, 25, 31), not to mention the Incarnation of Christ. Gnosticism also runs directly counter to the thinking of St. Thomas Aquinas, as G. K. Chesterton once stated with such elegance:

> Nobody will begin to understand the Thomist philosophy, or indeed the Catholic philosophy, who does not realize that the primary and fundamental part of it is entirely the praise of Life, the praise of Being, the praise of God as the Creator of the World.[184]

**54. Iconoclasm.** This is the heresy of the icon (image) smashers who gained prominence in the Eastern Church in the seventh and eighth centuries. Some cite the influence of the then-new religion of Islam, in which any kind of picture or sculpture of the human form was considered idolatry, although some earlier Christians held similar views. At its peak in the eighth century, many monasteries and churches were pillaged, and religious art was destroyed, along with the relics of saints. In a sense, iconoclastic history repeated itself in the sixteenth century in parts of continental Europe at the time of the Reformation, and also in domains under the sway of King Henry VIII, self-proclaimed head of the Church of England, when monasteries and churches were looted and destroyed or converted to Protestant houses of worship after the religious art was removed.[185]

---

[184] Chesterton, *Saint Thomas Aquinas*, 105.
[185] Having just returned from a trip to Ireland, still fresh in my mind is a famous twelfth-century cathedral confiscated and

Within this author's lifetime, iconoclasms of sorts have arisen, at times within the Church; for example, when new churches built in the later decades of the twentieth century grew increasingly bereft of religious art. Sadly, we see the literal destruction of the art and architecture of Christianity and other religions in parts of the Middle East by radical Muslim extremists. Further, within our nation at the time I write, we see icons, especially statues, of prominent, though imperfect political figures in our nation's history being literally smashed or removed by those who consider themselves far more morally enlightened than those imperfect figures from our nation's past.

Those who think like Aquinas should consider his recommendation on the perfection of memory to form corporeal images of even abstract spiritual concepts because, "spiritual impressions easily slip from the mind, unless they be tied as it were to some corporeal image, because human knowledge has a greater hold on sensible objects."[186] The mnemonic images we are employing in this book are mental icons of sorts that help us grasp and hold on to important concepts bearing on our intellectual and spiritual life.

Icons of religious art recognize as well that the human intellect is fed by and uplifted toward God by the evidence of the

---

partially destroyed by the soldiers of Oliver Cromwell in 1530 and later converted to a Protestant cathedral. Crucifixes were replaced by crosses, and statues of saints and angels were removed as idolatrous—only to be replaced over the centuries with statues of political figures and wealthy benefactors! Thankfully, however, the iconoclasm was not complete, as the church is now adorned with beautiful stained-glass windows depicting scenes from the life of St. Patrick.

[186] Aquinas, *Summa Theologica*, II-II, Q. 49, a. 1.

senses. Catholics do not worship the statues in our churches or homes any more than we worship the pictures of our loved ones that we hang on our walls or carry in our wallets.

Beautiful statues and other religious artworks feed our senses, stir our hearts, and enkindle our love by reminding us of the greatness and love of the God whom those icons were crafted to magnify and glorify. Those who think like Aquinas will turn to Scripture as well for passages wherein God commanded the construction of religious icons (Exod. 25:18–20; 1 Chron. 28:18–19), including a symbolic foreshadowing of Jesus Christ (see Num. 21:8–9 and John 3:14).

**55. Jansenism.** Jansenius (Cornelius Otto Jansen; 1585–1638), was the Catholic bishop of Ypres in Flanders (now part of Belgium). In his book *Augustinus*, dedicated to St. Augustine, he argued that salvation came solely to the elect (those predestined by God to receive His saving grace), that free will played no role in salvation, and that Christ died not for all but only for the elect. These views bear some resemblance to the Calvinism of the Protestant John Calvin (1509–1564). In a bull of 1642, Pope Urban VII forbade people to read *Augustinus*, since it promoted doctrines that had previously been condemned by the Catholic Church. Nonetheless, Jansen's followers erected a Jansenist church in Utrecht, Holland, in 1723, and it exists to this day.

### Heresies and Half-Truths 6–10 (Locations 56–60)

Last, but not least, we will deal with our final five heresies. At location 56 we find a chair before a computer armoire — the chair on which I sat when this memory house was first constructed. Years ago, my study was relocated, and now I write from a more spacious desk designed just for writing, and it sits in another room. That is just a fact to put things into context, but now we must move back into the old study and into the realm of the imagination if we are to remember this last batch of heresies.

Now, upon said chair (56) sits not me but a rather large *manatee* holding a *key*. (Are you familiar with these "sea cows" that rather look like hefty porpoises or tusk-less walruses?) True to fact, in the armoire (57), where once sat a computer, now sits a TV, and it sometimes displays commercials for all kinds of cures and medications. We will imagine that a commercial on the screen is touting a new wonder drug that cures both *mono*nucleosis and foot and mouth disease. (In fact, since it will cure either foot, we'll think in terms of *feet* and mouth disease.) On another bookcase (58), next to the armoire, is a bundle of twigs, strings, and such stuff that you conclude must be a *nest or an ism*. Why use an abstract thing like an ism? Perhaps we've been memorizing so many isms that everything's beginning to look like one! If you're not happy with this suggestion and are familiar with Homer's wise old character Nestor, just picture him sitting on that bookcase as you exclaim in less-than-perfect grammar, *"Nestor is him!"* Moving along now to a last portrait on the wall (59) next to the doorway out, you see, for some reason, a painting of an *aging pelican*. And now to the last stop on this memory tour. You open the study's closet door (60), and out springs an opera singer who loudly belts out a *solo* with words that she reads straight out of *Scripture*. You surmise that perhaps she is singing the psalms.

To conclude then with our heresies, that *manatee* with a *key* is sitting in my old chair (56) to remind us of *Manicheanism*, an ancient species not of sea mammals but of Gnosticism. The miracle drug on TV in the armoire (57) cures both *mono* and *feet* to remind us of *Monophysitism*, which held Jesus Christ had but one (*mono*) nature (*physis*), denying His full humanity and full divinity. That *nest or ism* (or "*Nestor is him!*" if you prefer) sitting atop the bookcase (58) serves to remind us of the heresy of *Nestorianism*, which promulgated various erroneous ideas, including that the Blessed Mother was not truly the Mother of God, because she gave birth only to Christ's *human* nature, denying Church teaching that Jesus Christ is the Word Incarnate, one person with two natures, and that Mary gave birth not only to a nature, but to the person of Jesus Christ, the incarnate Son of God. Across the room, the portrait by the doorway (59) depicts a *pelican aging* to remind us of the sound of the name *Pelagianism*, which held, in effect, that we could earn our own way and fly into heaven even without God's grace. Our memory tour has reached its end at the study's closet (60). Surely that opera singer singing a *solo* from *Scripture* will call to our minds the heresy of *sola Scriptura*, that pillar of Protestantism that forgets that "the church of the living God" is "the pillar and bulwark of the truth" (1 Tim. 3:15), the pillar and bulwark that provided the Bible itself, under the Holy Spirit's guidance, with its table of contents.

| Location | Image | Heresy |
| --- | --- | --- |
| 56. Chair before armoire | Manatee with a key | Manicheanism |
| 57. Armoire | Drug on TV for mono and feet | Monophysitism |
| 58. Bookcase | Nest or ism (or Homer's Nestor) | Nestorianism |

| Location | Image | Heresy |
| --- | --- | --- |
| 59. Portrait | Pelican aging | Pelagianism |
| 60. Closet door | Soloist sings Scripture | *sola Scriptura* |

**56. Manicheanism.** Taking its name from its Persian founder, Mani (216–274), this religion was a variant of Gnosticism and a precursor to Catharism. It presented itself as in perfect accord with reason and as the logical synthesis of other world religions, comprising elements of Zoroastrianism, which proclaimed dual gods of good and evil, ancient Babylonian mythology, Buddhist moral principles, and some distorted Christian principles. Jesus was seen as a "suffering savior," but rather than the Word Incarnate, He was regarded as a manifestation of "cosmic light" that was imprisoned in fleshly matter. Manicheanism is important in Christian history partly because of one very prominent former Manichean turned devout Catholic Christian, St. Augustine of Hippo (354–430).

Thomistic thought, as we've seen, is poles from Manicheanism, since it recognizes the goodness of the matter and spirit in which God made us as ensouled bodies. Further, the Word Himself was willing to take on a body for our sakes. Do you recall the time when Thomas was so lost in thought at the table of St. Louis, King of France, that he smashed down his mighty mitt upon the table and bellowed out, "And *that* will settle the Manicheans!" Perhaps Thomas's arguments did indeed settle them. At least we don't see a formal Manichean religion in our world today, though various elements of *gnostic* thought remain.

**57. Monophysitism.** This heretical view was espoused by Eutyches (378–456), an archimandrite (superior of a monastery) outside the great walled city of Constantinople. Monophysitism proposed that Christ had only one (*mono*) nature (*physis*) after the Incarnation. Christ, in this view, was not fully God and fully man because it was believed that "the human nature ceased to exist as such in Christ when the divine person of God's Son assumed it" (CCC 467). It was a variant of another form of monophysitism called *Apollinarism* or *Apollinarianism* espoused earlier by Syrian bishop Apollinaris (310–390), who held that Jesus could not have had a human mind. When Apollinarianism was condemned at the First Council of Constantinople in 381, it was said that the heresy portrayed Christ as *tertium quid*, a "third thing" neither man nor God. Eutyches's later version of monophysitism arose in response to, and as an overreaction to, the previous heresy of *Nestorianism*, which we will flesh out below.

**58. Nestorianism.** This heretical view was espoused by Nestorius (386–451), archbishop of Constantinople. He denied the validity of Mary's title *Theotokos* (God-bearer or Mother of God) by arguing that she gave birth only to Christ's *human* nature. Nestorius argued that she should actually be referred to as *Christotokos* (Christ-bearer or Mother of Christ). At the Council of Ephesus in 431, St. Cyril of Alexandria responded: "If any one does not confess that the Emmanuel (Christ) in truth is God and that on this account the Holy Virgin is the Mother of God (*Theotokos*)—since according to the flesh she brought forth the Word of God made flesh—let him be anathema." The dogma confirms that Mary was truly a mother, giving birth not to just a "nature" but to a human being who was the Second Person of the Trinity. And so, it's not just about an appropriate honorific for Mary; it's about safeguarding the full meaning of the Incarnation. Nestorianism was condemned at the Council of Ephesus in 431, and Monophysitism was condemned twenty years later at the Council of Chalcedon.

Thomas explained these issues in great depth in the *Summa Theologica*, part III, in fifty-nine questions with hundreds of articles addressing Christ, including the thirty-six articles of questions 2 through 6. He also addressed these issues sublimely in his explications of the first verses of John's Gospel in his *Commentary on the Gospel of John*.

*The Catechism of the Catholic Church* explains these issues at length in paragraphs 464–478 and provides a terse summary in paragraphs 479–483. To summarize briefly, it teaches that the Word of God become incarnate and assumed human nature without loss of His divine nature, being true God and true man with *two natures*, one divine and one human, united in the *one person* of God's son with a human intellect and will perfectly attuned to His divine intellect and will that He has in common with the Father and Holy Spirit. In sum: "The Incarnation is therefore the mystery of the wonderful union of the divine and human natures in the one person of the Word" (483).

**59. Pelagianism.** The British theologian Pelagius (360–420) promulgated a heresy that is in some respects the polar opposite of Calvinist and Jansenist views that would spread many centuries later. Whereas Calvin and Jansenius would, in effect, overemphasize our innate sinfulness as expounded in St. Augustine's writings on original sin, Pelagius nearly completely discounted it. Whereas the Jansenists would deny the power of our cooperation with God's grace through the use of our free will, Pelagius held that, in effect, we could raise ourselves to heaven by our own bootstraps, God's grace providing just an extra, nonessential boost! Pelagius, influenced by Greek philosophers, including the Stoics, who had no notion of original sin, held that we are born morally neutral but can attain heaven by following the model and example of Christ through the exercise of our own natural powers and virtues.

At the Council of Carthage in 418, Pelagianism was condemned in a series of propositions that make clear the reality of sin and the need for God's grace for the forgiveness of past sins, the avoidance of future sins, and even for the performance of good works.

St. Thomas addresses the necessity of grace again and again, specifically in the ten articles of question 109 in part I of the *Summa Theologica*: "The Necessity of Grace."

**60. Sola Scriptura.** I refer to this heresy as *sola Scriptura* rather than as a last ism, though it could be cast as either *Biblicism* or *Protestantism*, because it refers to the foundational Protestant view that "solely Scripture" or "the Bible alone" is the infallible guide to faith. The dissident English Catholic priest John Wycliffe (ca. 1320–1384) was among the first to spread this view, which denied the teaching authority of the Catholic Church through the pope and the Magisterium, and it led to the doctrine of private interpretation of Scripture under each person's guidance by the Holy Spirit. That doctrine should seem rather disconcerting on the face of it. Consider the vast number of contradictory and conflicting interpretations the same Holy Spirit apparently guides different people of different Protestant denominations toward in matters as vital as what we must do to be saved and whether, once saved, we can lose our salvation. It also leads to conflict over infant Baptism, and the nature and validity of all of the sacraments, including Christ's Real Presence in the Eucharist.

This subject is vast. A great many books have been written on the topic of *sola Scriptura*, and I've even included a chapter about it in one of my books.[187] To make a very long story short, fatal to this doctrine is the fact that the Catholic Church, founded by Christ upon the rock of Peter (Matt. 16:18), existed hundreds of years before the Church, with the Holy Spirit's guidance, pronounced the canon of books that the New Testament would comprise (its table of contents). Further, the Bible itself does not teach the doctrine of *sola Scriptura*, and, indeed, it identifies "the pillar and bulwark of the truth" as "*the church* of the living God" (1 Tim. 3:15, italics added).

As for thinking like Aquinas on this essential issue, anyone immersed in St. Thomas's writings will recognize his astonishing knowledge and love of Scripture. There are multiple scriptural references in virtually every article of the *Summa Theologica*, for example. His magnificent *Catena Aurea*, or *Golden Chain*, consists of the text of the Gospels accompanied by line-by-line commentaries by dozens of Western and Eastern Church Fathers and Doctors (which some scholars believe Thomas dictated from memory), and among his own most sublime books is his *Commentary on the Gospel of John*. Yet this angelic lover of the truth of Scripture was always a lover of that truth's "pillar and bulwark" as well, writing: "The Universal Church cannot err, since she is governed by the Holy Ghost, who is the Spirit of Truth."[188]

---

[187] Kevin Vost, *Memorize the Reasons: Defending the Faith with the Catholic Art of Memory* (San Diego: Catholic Answers Press, 2013), chap. 9.

[188] *Summa Theologica*, II-II, Q. 1, art. 90.

# Mnemonic Master Table

*If Simonides was the inventor of the art of memory, and "Tullius" its teacher, Thomas Aquinas became something like its patron saint.*

—Frances A. Yates, *The Art of Memory*

| Location | Image | Meaning |
| --- | --- | --- |
| 1. Front Door | Roosevelt speaks slowly; stick | Listen and think before you speak. |
| 2. Doormat | Prayerful hands emit sparks | Live a life of virtue and prayer. |
| 3. Glass panel | Thomas studies in cell; wine bottles | Learn to love the joys of studying. |
| 4. Portrait | Friends smile over book, then argue | Be friendly, but not too friendly. |
| 5. Gun rack | Globe entangles fingers | Don't let worldly things keep you from higher thoughts. |

# How to Think Like Aquinas

| Location | Image | Meaning |
| --- | --- | --- |
| 6. Center of foyer | Christ and saints | Imitate Christ, the saints, and the sages. |
| 7. Chandelier | Tooth held and admired by Mnemosyne | Embrace and memorize important truths. |
| 8. Mirror | Book with legs stands under a power generator | Fully employ your powers of understanding. |
| 9. Cushioned bench | Cupboard rests on base with no ledge | Never cease seeking to build your knowledge base. |
| 10. Drawers | Mentalist fails at trick | Exert your intellect to the max, but know that your powers are not limitless. |
| 11. Center of living room | Man, with vacuum, no, stick | *Argumentum ad baculum* |
| 12. Picture window | Archaeologist and *Homo sapiens* | *Argumentum ad hominem* |
| 13. Sofa | Man ignores ant | *Argumentum ad ignorantiam* |

# Mnemonic Master Table

| Location | Image | Meaning |
|---|---|---|
| 14. Coffee table | Miser with cord and money bag | *Argumentum ad misericordium* |
| 15. Big-screen TV | Popular actors argue | *Argumentum ad populum* |
| 16. Living-room fireplace | Man argues with barracuda | *Argumentum ad verecundiam* |
| 17. Living-room doorway | Dictator and simpleton | *Dicto simpliciter* |
| 18. Dining-room doorway | False dice | False dichotomy |
| 19. Head of table | Jeans fall, and you see | Genetic fallacy |
| 20. Center of table | Pacing military general | Hasty generalization |
| 21. Wall thermometer | Hyper people bowling | Hyperbole |
| 22. Seat on right | Petite principal | *Petitio principii* |
| 23. Foot of table | Posting hockey puck | *Post hoc, ergo propter hoc* |

# How to Think Like Aquinas

| Location | Image | Meaning |
|---|---|---|
| 24. Seat on left | Red herring | Red herring |
| 25. Doorway to family room | Quotation out of con's text | Quotation out of context |
| 26. Dresser | Dresser is slanting | Slanting |
| 27. Television | Preacher's special pleading | Special pleading |
| 28. Closet | Stereo typing | Stereotyping |
| 29. Weight bench | Straw man lifting | Straw man |
| 30. Pool table | UN distributes middle term paper | Undistributed middle term |
| 31. Recliner | A man says, "Gee, I don't know" | Agnosticism |
| 32. Couch | Man, with a thesis there is no God | Atheism |
| 33. Doorway out | Convict with sequins | Consequentialism |
| 34. Baptismal font | Construction worker | Constructivism |

| Location | Image | Meaning |
|---|---|---|
| 35. Front center | Man consumes huge meal | Consumerism |
| 36. Altar | Emotional priest crying | Emotivism |
| 37. Confessional | People with Bibles bow before Fido | Fideism |
| 38. Front pew right | Your favorite history teacher | Historicism |
| 39. Back of church | Cardsharp says, "I deal isms!" | Idealism |
| 40. Start of center aisle | Child: "one nation, individual" | Individualism |
| 41. Study door | Saleslady with material | Materialism |
| 42. Short bookcase | Southerner: "It's ma turn for Isms." | Modernism |
| 43. Tall bookcase | Knees, heels, nothing | Nihilism |
| 44. Presents on top of case | Trainer to dog: "No mints, Al!" | Nominalism |

| Location | Image | Meaning |
|----------|-------|---------|
| 45. Picture | Post office: "Ma turn" again | Postmodernism |
| 46. First chair | "P" rag, mat | Pragmatism |
| 47. Tall lamp | Reducing-machine belt | Reductionism |
| 48. Second chair | All your relatives | Relativism |
| 49. Footrest | Scientist hunched over microscope | Scientism |
| 50. Picture window | Skippers say, "Skip this ism!" | Skepticism |
| 51. Globe | Hitler touts Aryanism | Arianism |
| 52. Bookcase | Cath arisen from bed | Catharism |
| 53. Doorway out | Heretic: "G no stick!" | Gnosticism |
| 54. Diplomas | Heretic: "I cannot class them!" | Iconoclasm |
| 55. Picture | Jan's son | Jansenism |

| Location | Image | Meaning |
| --- | --- | --- |
| 56. Chair before armoire | Manatee with a key | Manicheanism |
| 57. Armoire | Drug on TV for mono and feet | Monophysitism |
| 58. Bookcase | Nest or ism (or Homer's Nestor) | Nestorianism |
| 59. Portrait | Pelican aging | Pelagianism |
| 60. Closet door | Soloist sings Scripture | *sola Scriptura* |

# About the Author

Kevin Vost, Psy.D., obtained his doctor of psychology degree in clinical psychology from Adler University in Chicago with internship and dissertation research at the Southern Illinois University School of Medicine, Alzheimer's Center, Memory and Aging Clinic. His dissertation was entitled "Executive Functioning in Early Alzheimer's Disease" and his master's thesis from Sangamon State University was entitled "Memory Strategy Instruction and the Internalization of Higher Psychological Processes in Adolescence."

Dr. Vost has taught psychology and gerontology at Aquinas College in Nashville, the University of Illinois at Springfield, MacMurray College, and Lincoln Land Community College. He has also served as a Research Review Committee member for American Mensa and as an advisory-board member for the International Association of Resistance Trainers. In 2017, Kevin and his wife, Kathy, became lay Dominican Associates with the Dominican Sisters of Springfield, Illinois.

Dr. Vost is the author of more than a dozen Catholic books, has appeared on hundreds of Catholic radio and television broadcasts, and has traveled across the United States and Ireland, giving talks on the themes of his books. When home, he continues to drink great draughts of coffee while studying timeless, Thomistic tomes in the company of his wife, their two sons, and their two dogs.

# Bibliography

Adler, Mortimer Jerome. *Intellect: Mind over Matter*. New York: Macmillan, 1990.

Aquinas, St. Thomas. *The Aquinas Catechism: A Simple Explanation of the Catholic Faith by the Church's Greatest Theologian*. Manchester, NH: Sophia Institute Press, 2000.

————. *Aquinas on Human Nature*. Edited by Thomas S. Hibbs. Indianapolis, IN: Hackett, 1999.

————. *Commentary on Aristotle's* De Anima. Notre Dame, IN: Dumb Ox Books, 1994.

————. *Commentary on Boethius'* On the Trinity. St. Isidore Forum. https://isidore.co/aquinas/english/BoethiusDeTr.htm#L22.

————. *De Magistro*. In *The Philosophy of Teaching of St. Thomas Aquinas*. Edited by Mary Helen Mayer. Milwaukee: Bruce, 1929.

————. *Summa Contra Gentiles*. Translated by Anton C. Pegis. Notre Dame, IN: University of Notre Dame Press, 1975.

————. *Summa Theologica*. 5 vols. Westminster, MD: Christian Classics, 1981.

Aquinas, St. Thomas. *The Aquinas Prayer Book: The Prayers and Hymns of St. Thomas Aquinas*. Edited by Robert Anderson and Johann Moser. Manchester, NH: Sophia Institute Press, 2000.

Aquinas, St. Thomas, and Aristotle. *Commentary on the Nicomachean Ethics*. Notre Dame, IN: Dumb Ox Books, 1993.

Aquinas, St. Thomas, and Victor White. *How to Study: Being the Letter of St. Thomas Aquinas to Brother John, De Modo Studendi*. Oxford: Oxonian Press, 1953.

Aristotle. *The Complete Works of Aristotle: The Revised Oxford Translation*. Edited by Jonathan Barnes. Princeton, NJ: Princeton University Press, 1984.

Bass, Clarence, and Carol Bass. *Take Charge: Fitness at the Edge of Science*. Albuquerque: Clarence Bass' Ripped Enterprises, 2013.

Blum, Christopher O., and Joshua Hochschild. *A Mind at Peace: Reclaiming an Ordered Soul in the Age of Distraction*. Manchester, NH: Sophia Institute Press, 2017.

Boucher, Anthony. "The Quest for Saint Aquin." In *Science Fiction Hall of Fame*, edited by Lester del Rey, 458–476. New York: Avon, 1971.

Brennan, Robert Edward. *Thomistic Psychology: A Philosophic Analysis of the Nature of Man*. New York: Macmillan, 1941.

Carr, Nicholas. "How Smartphones Hijack Our Minds." *Wall Street Journal*, October 6, 2017.

Carr, Nicholas G. *The Shallows: What the Internet Is Doing to Our Brains*. New York: W. W. Norton, 2010.

Carruthers, Mary. *The Book of Memory: A Study of Memory in Medieval Culture*. New York: Cambridge University Press, 1990.

Catholic Church. *Catechism of the Catholic Church*. New York: Doubleday, 1995.

Chesterton, G. K. *Saint Thomas Aquinas: The Dumb Ox*. New York: Doubleday Image, 1956.

Chi, M.T.H. "Knowledge Structures and Memory Development." In *Children's Thinking: What Develops?* Edited by Robert S. Siegler. New York: L. Erlbaum Associates, 1978.

Chrysostom, St. John. *Homilies on Matthew*. New Advent. http://www.newadvent.org/fathers/200115.htm.

Climacus, St. John. *The Ladder of Divine Ascent*. New York: Paulist Press, 1982.

Dawkins, Richard. *The God Delusion*. Boston: Houghton Mifflin, 2008.

Dondaine, Antoine. *Les Secretaires De Saint Thomas*. 2 vols. Rome: Editori di S. Tommaso, 1956.

Epictetus. *Epictetus: Discourses Books I-II, the Enchiridion*. Translated by William Abbott Oldfather. Cambridge, MA: Harvard University Press, 2000.

John Paul II, Pope. Encyclical letter *Fides et Ratio* (September 14, 1998).

Leo XIII, Pope. Encyclical *Aeterni Patris* (August 4, 1879).

Lipka, Michael. "10 Facts about Atheists." Pew Research Center, June 1, 2016. http://www.pewresearch.org/fact-tank/2016/06/01/10-facts-about-atheists/.

McGuff, Doug, and John R. Little. *Body by Science: A Research Based Program for Strength Training, Body Building, and Complete Fitness in 12 Minutes a Week*. New York: McGraw-Hill, 2009.

Mele, Alfred R. *Free: Why Science Hasn't Disproved Free Will*. New York: Oxford University Press, 2014.

Mioni, Anthony J., ed. *The Popes against Modern Errors*. Rockford, IL: TAN Books, 1999.

Mueller, John D. *Redeeming Economics: Rediscovering the Missing Element.* Wilmington, DE: ISI Books, 2010.

Murray, Charles A. *Human Accomplishment: The Pursuit of Excellence in the Arts and Sciences, 800 BC to 1950.* New York: HarperCollins, 2003.

Murray, Paul. *Aquinas at Prayer: The Bible, Mysticism and Poetry.* London: Bloomsbury Continuum, 2013.

————. *The New Wine of Dominican Spirituality: A Drink Called Happiness.* New York: Burns and Oates, 2006.

Olds, Jacqueline, and Richard Schwartz. *The Lonely American: Drifting Apart in the Twenty-First Century.* Boston: Beacon Press, 2009.

Pius IX. Motu proprio *Doctoris Angelici* (June 29, 1914).

Pius X, Pope. *On Modernism.* In *The Popes against Modern Errors.* Rockford, IL: TAN Books, 1999.

Pius XI, Pope. Encyclical *Studiorem Ducem* (June 29, 1923).

Pius XII, Pope. *Humani Generis.* In *The Popes against Modern Errors.* Rockford, IL: TAN Books, 1999.

Rand, Ayn. *Capitalism: The Unknown Ideal.* New York: New American Library, 1965.

Ratey, John J., and Eric Hagerman. *Spark: The Revolutionary New Science of Exercise and the Brain.* New York: Little, Brown, 2008.

Ratzinger, Joseph Cardinal. Homily at the Vatican basilica, April 18, 2005. http://www.vatican.va/gpII/documents/homily-pro-eligendo-pontifice_20050418_en.html.

Raymond of Capua, Blessed. *The Life of St. Catherine of Siena.* Charlotte, NC: St. Benedict Press, 2006.

Redpath, Peter. *The Moral Psychology of St. Thomas Aquinas: An Introduction to Ragamuffin Ethics.* St. Louis: En Route Books, 2017.

# Bibliography

Sertillanges, A. G., and Mary Ryan. *The Intellectual Life: Its Spirit, Conditions, Methods.* Westminster, MD: Newman Press, 1948.

Shaughnessy, M., and Mary L. White. "Making Macro Memorable: The Method of Loci Mnemonic Technique in the Economics Classroom." *Journal of Economics and Finance Education* 11, no. 2 (Winter 2012): 131–141.

Snider, Marie. "Miracle-Gro for Brains." *Exercise Revolution* (blog), March 2008. http://johnratey.typepad.com/blog/2008/03/miracle-gro-for.html.

Sokal, Alan D., and J. Bricmont. *Fashionable Nonsense: Postmodern Intellectuals' Abuse of Science.* New York: Picador USA, 1998.

Tugwell, Simon, ed. *Albert and Thomas: Selected Writings.* New York: Paulist Press, 1988.

Vost, Kevin. *The Catholic Guide to Loneliness: How Science and Faith Can Help Us Understand It, Grow from It, and Conquer It.* Manchester, NH: Sophia Institute Press, 2017.

———. *Fit for Eternal Life: A Christian Approach to Working Out, Eating Right, and Building the Virtues of Fitness in Your Soul.* Manchester, NH: Sophia Institute Press, 2007.

———. *The Four Friendships: From Aristotle to Aquinas.* Angelico Press, 2018.

———. *Memorize the Faith! (and Most Anything Else): Using the Methods of the Great Catholic Medieval Memory Masters.* Manchester, NH: Sophia Institute Press, 2006.

———. *Memorize the Reasons: Defending the Faith with the Catholic Art of Memory.* San Diego: Catholic Answers Press, 2013.

———. *The One-Minute Aquinas: The Doctor's Quick Answers to Fundamental Questions.* Manchester, NH: Sophia Institute Press, 2014.

————. *Unearthing Your Ten Talents: A Thomistic Guide to Spiritual Growth through the Virtues and the Gifts*. Manchester, NH: Sophia Institute Press, 2009.

Vost, Kevin, Shane Kapler, and Peggy Bowes. *Tending the Temple*. Waterford, MI: Bezalel Books, 2011.

Yates, Frances Amelia. *The Art of Memory*. Chicago: University of Chicago Press, 1966.

# Sophia Institute

Sophia Institute is a nonprofit institution that seeks to nurture the spiritual, moral, and cultural life of souls and to spread the Gospel of Christ in conformity with the authentic teachings of the Roman Catholic Church.

Sophia Institute Press fulfills this mission by offering translations, reprints, and new publications that afford readers a rich source of the enduring wisdom of mankind.

Sophia Institute also operates two popular online Catholic resources: CrisisMagazine.com and CatholicExchange.com.

*Crisis Magazine* provides insightful cultural analysis that arms readers with the arguments necessary for navigating the ideological and theological minefields of the day. *Catholic Exchange* provides world news from a Catholic perspective as well as daily devotionals and articles that will help you to grow in holiness and live a life consistent with the teachings of the Church.

In 2013, Sophia Institute launched Sophia Institute for Teachers to renew and rebuild Catholic culture through service to Catholic education. With the goal of nurturing the spiritual, moral, and cultural life of souls, and an abiding respect for the role and work of teachers, we strive to provide materials and programs that are at once enlightening to the mind and ennobling to the heart; faithful and complete, as well as useful and practical.

Sophia Institute gratefully recognizes the Solidarity Association for preserving and encouraging the growth of our apostolate over the course of many years. Without their generous and timely support, this book would not be in your hands.

www.SophiaInstitute.com
www.CatholicExchange.com
www.CrisisMagazine.com
www.SophiaInstituteforTeachers.org

Sophia Institute Press® is a registered trademark of Sophia Institute.
Sophia Institute is a tax-exempt institution as defined by the
Internal Revenue Code, Section 501(c)(3). Tax I.D. 22-2548708.